Endorsements for *Marketing Yourself*

"The most actionable marketing book I've ever seen! Great step-by-step instructions with memorable examples. Loved it."

— Derek Sivers, author of *Anything You Want*

"There are books that you read — and there are books that you USE. Caelan has written the second kind. Consider this your action guide, implementation kit, and field manual for marketing success. Page after page of money-making ideas that work and last."

— David Newman, author of *Do It! Marketing* and
Do It! Speaking

"Caelan has done what is not always possible for books about branding and marketing. He's created something practical and instantly applicable. This book is a must-read for anyone starting out and looking for a step-by-step process."

— Donna McGeorge, bestselling author of
The 25 Minute Meeting

"Personal branding literature is a genre unto itself these days, but *Marketing Yourself* is by far the most well-crafted, researched, and useful I've ever read. Caelan provides frameworks that you can employ to boost your brand right away, literally, paint-by-the-numbers. It's packed with great examples, so I don't feel like I'm left hanging with a good idea but no coaching. It's all there. From values to website, here you will find everything you need to look great in the world without ever feeling overwhelmed."

— Joshua Waldman, author of
Job Searching with Social Media for Dummies

"Caelan's a genius. His background and his unique combination of skills make him an expert in personal marketing. He is generous with his knowledge in these pages, and he tells great stories."

— Kathleen Celmins, author of *Mindstorms*

"Assuming you would like more people to know about what you are doing or creating, this book is 100% worth your time. It'll help the world market smarter, not harder."

— Chad Littlefield, author of *Ask Powerful Questions*

"Caelan is one of those rare authors who seems to deeply understand what we as entrepreneurs need. His mix of insights, case studies, and personal stories had me fully engaged throughout the book, and I now have a notepad full of practical takeaways to implement."

— Vince Warnock, author of *Chasing the Insights*

"Caelan has taken an extensive topic and broken it down into digestible key concepts that will help you understand how to grow your brand. His vast experience, gift of storytelling, and library of tools and templates make this resource a top pick for anyone wanting to elevate their personal brand to the next level."

— Bryan Whitefield, author of *Persuasive Advising*

"*Marketing Yourself* is a fabulously practical guide to growing your ability to market yourself, and if you implement even a portion of the ideas shared in this book, your value is certain to grow."

— Col Fink, author of *Tribes*

"This book gives you an actionable process so your audience can see you, hear you, and find you."

— Jackie Barrie

"Caelan Huntress oozes charisma and adventure. Mix in strong shots of curiosity, communication wizardry and practicality, and you'll understand the magic of *Marketing Yourself*. It combines clear advice with compelling stories, offered up by someone who walks the talk."

— Rebecca Sutherns, Ph.D.

"This book contains a number of powerful tools and techniques for anyone trying to grow their business. I believe the most expensive cost in business is the learning curve. The more you know, the less you guess. And guessing is expensive. READ this book and avoid funding the ever-painful learning curve in your business."

— Mike Brian

"This is the best marketing book I've ever read! Caelan breaks down complicated marketing principles into simple, actionable steps. He helps clarify your business vision and purpose and then gives easy steps on how to share it with the world. I highly recommend this book to anyone in business, whether you are a new entrepreneur or have been in business for 30 years."

— Renee Spears

"What a great read for entrepreneurs keen to get the word out there but with no idea where to start. What I love about this book is how intensely practical it is, without the marketing-talk or fluff that can really put you off marketing yourself! And let's face it, if he can market himself from the jungle, you can do it from your lounge room."

— Rebecca Houghton

"If you're looking for a practical, no-nonsense approach to establishing yourself as an expert, this is the book for you. Caelan provides easy-to-follow steps that make it impossible not to take action and see results."

— Taylorr Payne

MARKETING YOURSELF

How To Elevate Your Personal Platform to the Next Level

CAELAN HUNTRESS

Marketing Yourself

Stellar Platforms Publishing
4931 SW 76th Ave. #108
Portland, OR 97225

MarketingYourselfBook.com

Editor: Kim Ledgerwood, The Right Word
Interior Layout: Fusion Creative Works
Cover Design: Colibrian on 99 Designs
Author Photo: Elizabeth Jenkins Photography

Library of Congress Control Number:
Paperback ISBN: 979-8-9864617-0-0
ebook ISBN: 979-8-9864617-1-7
Audiobook ISBN: 979-8-9864617-2-4

10 9 8 7 6 5 4 3 2 1
First Edition, 2022
Printed in the United States of America

Dedication

This book is dedicated to every entrepreneur, industry expert, and passionate professional who is willing to stake their personal reputation on their own success.

Table of Contents

Preface

This book was written in the early 2020s by someone who spent a decade traveling the world as a digital nomad and running a business from his laptop.

Many of the concepts and techniques that worked well during this time period may be outdated, antiquated, or hopelessly unfashionable by the time you read this.

I learned these lessons as a service provider, helping experts and entrepreneurs grow their businesses, as a digital marketer for hire. You may have a different type of business, or you may work for an employer. You might be a solopreneur, or have a small staff, or manage a large team. Wherever possible, I've tried to make the concepts general in nature, to focus on the fundamentals that may prove timeless. However, I often rely upon era-specific examples as methods to illustrate these universal ideas.

I apologize in advance for anything I reference that is now obsolete. If you have never had an email address, because Web 4.0 made identity redundant or something, please read this relic of the past as an homage to the era where I learned about marketing yourself.

— Caelan Huntress

Foreword

Marketing yourself is a personal journey. No matter what kind of business goals you've set for yourself, marketing yourself is still personal.

Many marketing books promote a single, linear path for marketing a personal or business brand. It's no wonder those types of marketing prescriptions don't work for most readers. There's no wiggle room. They're not the right fit for everyone. How could they be?

When I read Caelan's book, I gave a sigh of relief when I saw that he offered options for his readers. An element of choose-your-own-path is essential to marketing yourself in a way that feels aligned to who you are and what makes you unique. The tools, worksheets, and frameworks inside this book allow readers to find the path that's right for them, instead of trying to force readers onto one path that everyone else is crowding.

Both personally and professionally, Caelan's life has been an example of walking your own path. The stories he shares within these pages — hitchhiking across the country, busking for cash by playing his guitar, "hacking" his sales job, moving with his family across the world — are only a fraction of the colorful and adventure-filled life he's lived. He's connected with people from all walks of life, and he brings that multi-faceted perspective to his consulting, his courses, and this book.

Marketing Yourself

There's a difference between a marketing guru and a marketing consultant. Gurus pontificate. Consultants collaborate. Counting myself among the latter, I have a deep respect for fellow consultants, like Caelan, who are resourceful enough to offer options instead of dictums. This book is your self-guided journey to doing the same thing for yourself.

As a communication coach and influence consultant, I know what goes on behind the scenes when a founder refreshes their marketing message. So, to help you get into the best mindset for this journey you're about to take, I'd like to remind you of two things ...

1) Let this be a creative process.

Your first answers to the exercises don't need to be polished. In fact, they probably shouldn't be. Let this book and its worksheets be your sandbox. Play! The freer you are in your answers, the more your marketing message will feel like you.

2) Let your future self speak.

Imposter syndrome is a real thing, even for highly successful people. In fact, in my experience, it's the people who care the most about their message and their clients who struggle the most with imposter syndrome. Narcissists are the ones who bulldoze through without much second-guessing. So, if you start to feel any resistance from imposter syndrome, let those be the moments you let your future self speak! Transport yourself to five years from now, when you've accomplished your goals and are living the personal and professional life you've envisioned. What would that person say? How would they answer these questions?

Your unique path to marketing yourself is within these pages, and you have a fantastic guide in Caelan to accompany you along the way.

Enjoy!

— Sharí Alexander, Communication Coach & Influence Strategist

Introduction

Marketing Yourself Is What Elevates You

Figure out who you are, and do it on purpose.

— Dolly Parton

Nobody elevates their personal platform by staying quiet, bland, or unseen. If you have something to say or something to sell, marketing yourself is how you attract an audience, spread your message, and sell your wares.

Earning and maintaining the attention of an audience was my very first craft. My teenage years were spent doing Shakespeare in the Park. The first paycheck I earned came from working as a carney in a funhouse. After that, I ran away and joined the circus, performing as a juggler and an acrobat. The stage was where I came of age, so it's where I've always felt the most at home.

After studying an ancient form of Italian street performance at the Dell'Arte International School of Physical Theatre, I started having kids. Shortly after, I learned how difficult it is to support a family as a performer (in America, no less). Like many other ex-actors, I gravitated to jobs that allowed me to monetize my charisma: first as a waiter, then as a salesperson, and finally as a marketer.

Through all three of these phases of my career, my success came from learning the foundational techniques of marketing yourself.

Waiting tables showed me that people tip better when they've had a low-maintenance, enjoyable experience. In a fancy dining room, I could make an expensive meal worthwhile by meeting my customers' highest expectations. I had to learn quickly how my customers wanted to be treated — and then treat them that way. I found that a customer is more likely to pay well, return later, and make recommendations to others if you're good at marketing yourself to them while you have their attention.

Selling taught me that revenue is a numbers game. If you can find a formula that gives predictable results, you can focus on the inputs you control to get the output you want. When I was working the phones in a boiler room, I was taught to track my calls with paper clips. Every phone call earned another paper clip in the jar on my desk. Recording my activity, I observed that an average of one out of every 25 calls turned into a sale. I decided to average 75 phone calls a day to average three daily sales, which earned my revenue goal. Selling is successful when you find and follow a simple formula.

Marketing taught me that people buy people. A buying decision doesn't depend on the features or benefits of what you sell. In fact, what you sell is almost inconsequential. Trust is what gives people the confidence to make a purchase, and marketing creates trust.

Runaway Solopreneur

When I left the United States with my young family, we had just lost everything. I'd lost my job, my house, my assets, and my credit. (Thanks, medical bills.) I couldn't get a job, so I was forced into becoming an entrepreneur, whether I liked it or not. We sold everything we owned to finance an international move to Costa Rica, a country that wouldn't bankrupt us for going to the hospital.

Introduction

I started my new business only months before becoming a digital nomad. As a sudden self-proprietor, I had to get my business working fast. I didn't have a lot of runway to figure things out at an easy pace. I had kids to feed, and my only plan for survival was marketing myself from a laptop in the middle of the jungle.

Thankfully, I had a unique overlap of skills that combined to make websites: I could write a little code, write good content, and design decent graphics. Not many people can do all three. I'm not an exceptional web designer, but I deliver solid work, and I'm great with people. When I started marketing myself, I found that I could financially support my family by doing two things: staying on message and staying in conversation with people who were likely to hire me.

Growing my business was always on my mind as I recovered from the financial trauma of American exceptionalism. Whenever people hired me to make WordPress websites for them, I would naturally transition any conversation about web design into lead generation, content marketing, and marketing strategy. This eventually became the core of my business, and I've spent the past decade helping experts and entrepreneurs set up smart marketing systems.

Through my digital marketing agency, Stellar Platforms, I've been fortunate enough to work with bestselling authors, syndicated radio hosts, and Hall of Fame public speakers. My best clients are people who want to share their message with a growing audience and don't want to get distracted from their core work by fumbling through their marketing messaging and automation technology.

Marketing Is Risky If It's Not Done Well

You might spend weeks, months, or years marketing yourself through trial and error, and still only be a substandard marketer. Which is a shame, because even though marketing might not be the focus of your business, your marketing effectiveness can often be the determining factor in your financial success.

What I've found in working with so many different types of individual entrepreneurs is that marketing yourself is inconsistent, takes a lot of time, and doesn't always justify the resources you put into it. You may have already spent too much time on a marketing tactic that isn't getting results, but you don't have the knowledge or the tools to try anything different.

When you finally find an effective system for marketing yourself, that's when you can focus your time and energy on doing your best work. There's a type of work that only you can do, in your voice, with your vision. If you can confine your sales and marketing activities to a couple of hours a week, then you can focus your time on your craft — and not on your marketing.

But first, you need a good platform.

The 4 Cornerstones of Your Personal Platform

Your personal platform is how you are known in the world, and it elevates you, supports you, and frames your work for your audience. You can expect to find success in your career in proportion to the size and stability of your platform.

A platform gives you a place to stand.

Right now, your platform might be big, or it might be small; it might be focused on your business or on your personality. Some platforms are sturdy and in good repair, while others are held together with duct tape and twine.

Marketing yourself from your own personal platform can make you feel uncomfortable. Putting on a persona is pretending, after all, and showing the world a curated expression of yourself can make you feel inauthentic, clumsy, or rude. But when it's done well, marketing yourself from a personal platform enables you to deliver your message directly to people who are eager to hear it.

A platform provides clarity over distance. With a solid platform underneath you, your audience can see you over the crowd, hear what you say, and know where to find you. A clear connection between you and your audience is the key to sustaining your growth and goals for decades.

Marketing yourself is the process of elevating your personal platform, and the height of your platform is determined by four cornerstones: Positioning, Profit, Strategy, and Systems.

Positioning (what you say) and Profit (what you sell) are the two external cornerstones of your platform. People can see these cornerstones when you have their attention. But there are also two internal cornerstones at the back of your platform — your Strategy and your Systems — and they're just as important. Each of these cornerstones contributes to your elevation.

FOUR CORNERSTONES

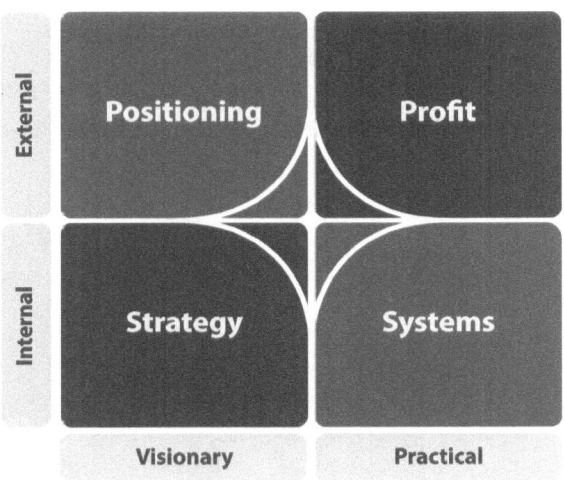

Is there one cornerstone that repeatedly demands your attention? If one of your cornerstones is small, unsteady, or weak, then your entire platform is always going to lean in that direction. Your attention will continually be distracted by the problems you face from this one cornerstone until you can strengthen it and raise it up to the same level as the others. If you want to elevate your platform to the next level, you can do that by working on your cornerstones, one at a time.

What's great about the internet is that you can work on your cornerstones from anywhere in the world. Millions of people have learned that you can run your own business in a manner that's aligned with your preferred lifestyle from anywhere you have Wi-Fi and caffeine. That means you can be doing the kinds of work you want to be doing, with global customers happy to do business with you, if you have a personal platform.

Helping people around the world elevate their personal platform is the work I do through Stellar Platforms. When appropriate, I will share stories from my own career, as well as case studies of clients with whom I've worked, and entrepreneurs that I admire.

At the end of each chapter, I'll refer you to workbooks I've created for producing content and marketing strategy. These workbooks can be found at https://MarketingYourselfBook.com/Workbooks.

If you find anything in this book that helps you on your journey, feel free to share on the hashtag **#MarketingYourselfBook.** I'd love to see your platform grow.

Cornerstone 1

Positioning

The world will ask you who you are, and if you do not know,
the world will tell you.

— Carl Jung

What you say about yourself, combined with what others say about you, becomes your Positioning. You can't completely control what others say about you, but you can influence it. The portion of your Positioning that you completely control is your message.

Your message is the interface between your ideas and the rest of the world. The reason you're trying to elevate your platform is so you can share your message and your meaning. Your message matters. It matters to you, and it matters to the people whose lives are changed by it.

Structuring your message so that it conveys the right meaning to the right people is the focus of your Positioning cornerstone. It may take some time to uncover your message in its purest form, to find a message that resonates strongly with who you are and who you want to be. It can take even longer to figure out how to shape that message so that it spreads. A new message needs to evolve, from what you want to say to what your audience has been waiting to hear. This takes time, consideration, experimentation, and revision.

A muddy message isn't clear enough for anyone to see very deeply into it, but articulating and clarifying your message enables you to share it widely.

Your first draft won't be your best draft, I promise you. Every time you tweak it, it will get better, so don't be disheartened if your message isn't perfect on the first try.

Expect experimentation.

Allow yourself to let go of what you've already accomplished, to stay open for a superior future to arrive. You get better with time — but only if you're willing to change.

Chapter 1

Your Personal Statement

*The only person you are destined to become
is the person you decide to be.*

— Ralph Waldo Emerson

Who do you think you are, anyway? If you've been marketing yourself for any length of time, it's likely you've already given some thought to this question. Chances are, you've already written a bio or an elevator pitch for yourself a time or two. And it's tricky, isn't it? It's hard to share all the different facets of yourself in a snappy little sentence. But a personal statement isn't supposed to detail every single one of your accomplishments from your entire life. The purpose is to give others a handle so they can grasp you.

There are three types of descriptions commonly used for positioning. A bio is the longer version of who you are, what you do, and why you're amazing. An elevator pitch is the medium-length version, and a personal statement is the shortest of the three. Each of these positioning assets can be used to get noticed, gain attention, and highlight your value to your customers.

An elevator pitch, as defined by Jeffrey Hayzlett, author of *Think Big, Act Bigger*, is 118 seconds. This is the average length of time of an elevator ride in New York City. If you're sharing a small, confined space with someone for a minute or two, you have enough time for a basic introduction. This brief window of time can be used to plant a seed that can sprout referrals for you for years to come.

Do people have to interpret your elevator pitch? Do they have to ask for clarification? If so, it's not done yet. Your elevator pitch should be one paragraph — or maybe two — that serves as a beacon for the people that you want to meet in the future.

A personal statement is like the headline of a flyer on a bulletin board. Bulletin boards are a mess. They collect random announcements from random people, all wanting to broadcast their message out into the world.

Think about the flyers that have gotten your attention in the past. Did you notice a flyer because it had long prose, describing many tiny details? Or was there one really powerful headline in big letters? Was it something particularly relevant to you? Did the flyer reference something you were already looking for?

You can manufacture that same kind of distinction (and gain quick attention with the right people) with your personal statement. The distillation of your bio (the longer written delivery) and your elevator pitch (the shorter verbal delivery) into a simple statement that is sticky, clear, and short becomes your personal statement.

- ✦ Sticky — easy to remember
- ✦ Clear — simple and direct
- ✦ Short — dazzles in a flash

Long, Medium, and Short Positioning

Your biography is a menu for the types of topics that you can discuss forever. These topics become the calling card for interviewers and members of the press who are looking for experts like you. A brief overview of your experience and accomplishments related to these topics is what makes your bio. Writing this once, and writing it well, will save you countless hours of writer's block in the future.

An elevator pitch can be given to anyone, and the right kinds of people will hear it as an invitation to work with you. Think of your elevator pitch as the key to the gatekeeper who answers the phone. When calling on a business to connect with a decision-maker, you often run into a gatekeeper. This person hears you out and decides whether or not to connect you with the boss. The right elevator pitch gets you access.

A personal statement is the shortest, most concentrated version of your elevator pitch and your bio. It should be easy to remember, easy to understand, and easy to endure. This makes it hard to forget and hard to interrupt.

You shouldn't make up these positioning assets on the spot. Your written bio and verbal elevator pitch are most effective if you articulate them in advance. When someone asks you to talk about yourself, which would you rather do? Recite (or copy/paste) a prepared statement, or fumble through an improvised introduction every single time?

When people are struggling to get their platform off the ground, the problem is often in the foundation, and a solid personal statement is what gives your platform stability. It's a signal to your future customers and collaborators. But remember, a personal statement doesn't need to include everything you've ever done. Think of it more like a highlight reel.

A tightly written personal statement does two things: it clearly articulates the types of people who find you valuable, and it describes the types of things you do for them. The problems you solve, and the solutions you provide. That's it. These are clearer signals to future customers than an exhaustive list of all your accomplishments.

The best personal statement that I have ever heard was from Cory Huff. Cory has a website called theabundantartist.com. When I met him in 2015 at Pioneer Nation, a conference for independent entrepreneurs making a living through their laptops, I asked him, "What do you do?"

He replied, "I help people sell their art online."

His personal statement was sticky, clear, and short. I immediately thought of everyone I knew who was an artist, struggling to sell their art online — and I sent every one of them to Cory's website. He has such a tightly defined market, and he's so clear about what he does for them, that it's easy for new customers to find him.

When people can quickly and easily understand who you help, what you do, and how you do it, great things happen. Chance meetings lead to new clients and customers showing up (seemingly) out of nowhere. The truth is, people can easily connect you to people they know (people who already want to hire someone like you) when your personal statement is sticky, clear, and short, like Cory's.

Using the simple formulas below, replace the words in CAPS to try out a new personal statement.

Personal Statement Formulas

"I help DEMOGRAPHIC
dealing with PROBLEM by SOLUTION."

"I help DEMOGRAPHIC OUTCOME
through METHOD."

"I provide SOLUTION
to people who are DEMOGRAPHIC and want OUTCOME."

A good personal statement can dramatically increase your referrals. By using a formula like the ones above, you clearly state the type of customer who finds you valuable, and specifically define what you do for them.

Life is not about finding yourself.
Life is about creating yourself.
— George Bernard Shaw

Personal Statement Examples

- ✦ *Adan Sensei helps people have a 15-minute conversation in their target language.*

- ✦ *Shay Rowbottom turns founders and executives into LinkedIn video creators.*

- ✦ *Max Menke helps companies, startups, and countries commercialize innovation and get products to market.*

- ✦ *Kelly Irving is a book editor and publishing strategist who helps authors make book ideas better.*

- ✦ *Bryan Whitefield helps organizations make smarter, faster decisions.*

- ✦ *Lisa Evans helps leaders transform their public speaking and storytelling skills for greater impact.*

- ✦ *Derek Edmond helps B2B companies generate results in search engines.*

- ✦ *Matt Church is a mentor and trusted advisor to thought leaders and global influencers.*

These personal statements are sticky, clear, and short. They're easy to remember, easy to understand, and hard to forget. Here's mine:

- ✦ *Caelan Huntress helps experts and entrepreneurs set up smart marketing systems.*

My personal statement clearly defines what I do and how I do it. You know after one quick read if I'm the type of person you hire or follow. I don't talk about my fire juggling skills or my blockchain proficiency because I don't want to muddy the message when I'm giving someone my introduction.

How a Personal Statement Gives You Momentum

The first few years in business are the hardest. You're trying to figure out how you make money, who you serve, what you're doing for them, and how to talk about it. After a while, people start coming to you out of nowhere. They talked with someone you barely remember, and they happen to be facing exactly the kind of problem that you're best suited to solve. Referrals become common. You don't have to hustle so hard.

Your personal statement plants seeds among your weak ties, and over time those seeds will sprout into referrals. Counterintuitively, the effectiveness of your reputation relies on the strength of your weak ties, not on your direct connections.

In his landmark sociology paper "The Strength of Weak Ties," Stanford professor and sociologist Mark Granovetter surveyed 282 workers in Boston and found that 84% of them had gotten their job through a weak-tie relationship.1 Weak ties are acquaintances who know you but aren't close to you. You may go weeks, months, or even years without speaking to one another, but you would answer their call or reply to their email.

Having a large circle of acquaintances, Granovetter argued, is better for discovering opportunities. Your weak ties talk with dozens (or hundreds) of people who aren't connected to you at all. Those weak ties can remember you when something relevant comes up in their wider network. Your close friends and family members — people who you see regularly — don't have access to an entirely separate network of people, but your weak ties do, and they may have heard something they can pass on to you.

---

1 Ian Leslie, "Why your 'weak tie' friendships may mean more than you think," The Life Project, BBC, last modified July 2, 2020, https://www.bbc.com/worklife/article/20200701-why-your-weak-tie-friendships-may-mean-more-than-you-think

If your personal statement is sticky, clear, and short, then your weak ties will continually share your work with their separate networks of contacts.

Copy-Paste Copywriting Process

One of the fastest ways I know to iterate your way to success is with copy-paste copywriting. This is the secret to being a good copywriter. I don't start content from scratch. I start with a formula. Sometimes I develop these formulas myself. Sometimes I reverse-engineer formulas from content I find out in the wilds of the internet. This is a simple process I've used for years to develop great content quickly.

1. Find the formula

2. Fill in the blanks

3. Fix the flow

4. Repeat

If I'm writing a bio for a client, for example, here's a formula I'd use:

> *NAME is the TITLE at COMPANY. She is a ADJECTIVE and ADJECTIVE ROLE, ROLE, and ROLE whose insight is grounded in over NUMBER years of experience as a successful ROLE, ROLE, and specialist in OUTCOME.*

In many of my Cornerstone Workbooks, you can double-click on words in CAPS to replace them with your own customized text. When I use this formula for myself, this is what I get:

> *Caelan Huntress is the Creative Director at Stellar Platforms. He is a brilliant and dynamic speaker, trainer, and business coach whose insight is grounded in over 15 years of experience as a successful stage performer, direct-response copywriter, and specialist in digital marketing automation.*

As you develop your own positioning for your platform, pay attention to the positioning of others. Take notes. And use formulas because they allow you to create your positioning content quickly.

ACTION STEPS FOR ELEVATING YOUR PLATFORM

Complete the exercises in the Cornerstone Workbooks at MarketingYourselfBook.com/workbooks:

SCAN ME

1. Use the first workbook's opening exercises to write about yourself, your audience, and your solution.

2. Write a bio (longer written version), an elevator pitch (shorter verbal version), and a personal statement (sticky, clear, and short).

3. Share your personal statement with friends and colleagues. Ask for feedback. Revise it a few times.

4. Change your headlines on your social profiles and website.

Chapter 2

Mission-Based Messaging

Marketing is no longer about the stuff you make,
but about the stories you tell.

— Seth Godin

What you say is more than just your words. Words are important because they align others to your mission, and your mission creates the best messaging.

In the most popular TED Talk of all time, "How great leaders inspire action," Simon Sinek famously challenges us to Start With Why. In his book with the same title, he says, "People don't buy what you do, they buy why you do it." He uses what he calls "The Golden Circle" to illustrate the three levels of meaning: Why, How, and What.

THE GOLDEN CIRCLE

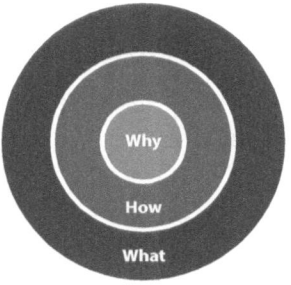

The problem, Sinek says, is that most people have this backward. They don't start with Why. They start talking about What they do, then they talk about How they do it, and they finally finish with Why that matters.

We do this a lot in marketing ourselves, too. Our "What" is how we introduce ourselves. "How" forms the backbone of our conversations. "Why" might end up on a brochure, but we don't start our marketing conversations there. That means we have to continually convince people to buy, when we could make it much easier on ourselves by enrolling advocates instead.

Creating Customers vs. Creating Advocates

There is a critical difference between buying a product and advocating for a mission. For example, parents like to buy college sweatshirts because they are advocates of the mission to educate their children. They don't care if the sweatshirt is $90 if it has the logo of their kid's school on it. The parents are buying the Why, not the fabric.

People will pay a premium price if they are also buying your mission.

When you enroll advocates, their enthusiasm for the mission becomes infectious. You can see this with individual solopreneurs selling their services, and also with massive companies that manage thousands of employees.

If a company has a clear mission, according to research done by Imperative, they are 54% more likely to retain employees for more than five years.[2] The employees of mission-driven organizations aren't just working for a check. They are also working for the mission. When

2 Aaron Hurst, "Purpose Trumps Cash + Other New Research Findings," Imperative, last modified July 19, 2016, https://www.imperative.com/post/ purpose-trumps-cash-other-new-research-findings

someone contributes to a mission, they are more likely to stick around when the going gets tough. The only people who will give everything they can to support the mission are true advocates.

Marketing Is About Values

Steve Jobs championed the mission of Apple when he said, "People with passion can change the world for the better." Marketing this mission goes beyond the technical specifications of the product or the price tag on the box. Apple customers are willing to pay a higher price, and it's not always because of the processing power or the flashy design. People pay more to buy Apple because they identify with the mission.

Several surveys have found that around 60% of millennials chose their workplace because of the company's mission. Younger generations are increasingly deciding where to work based on how well a company's mission aligns with their own values. This mindset also affects their buying decisions when they're considering whether to purchase from someone like you.

Case Study 1: Online Shoe Shopping or Shoes for Shoeless Children?

There are plenty of shoes available for sale on the internet, but TOMS Shoes is different. Their company mission is, "We're in business to improve lives," and they incorporate that mission into every transaction. For every pair of TOMS shoes you buy, they'll provide a pair of shoes to a child in need.

They help bring footwear to people who otherwise might not have it by leveraging your privilege. You're able to buy a brand-new pair of shoes and have them shipped right to your door. TOMS Shoes extends that privilege to others who can't. They're making the world a better place. It's part of their mission, part of their Why. In addition to keeping you well-shod, they also improve the world for shoeless kids.

Knowing that, do you really think people who buy TOMS Shoes are concerned that their purchase might cost a few dollars more? With strong mission-based messaging, price is not as important a factor in buying decisions.

Your Mission Helps People Make Decisions

When a customer aligns with your mission, their decisions are made differently. A lot of latitude can be given to a product or a service if you know that you're supporting a mission you agree with. If the shipping took a couple of extra days, or it cost a few more dollars, it's not that big of a deal — because you're supporting a mission. You're supporting a Why.

Your Why becomes a filter all of your decisions can flow through. When you have your Why at the forefront, people can easily distinguish between you and other options available, and decisions can be made clearly in alignment with more values than just money.

Case Study 2: Cookie Sales Champion or World Traveler?

Markita Andrews won a competition for selling the most Girl Scout cookies in a single year. She was raised by her aunt, who made a deal with her. If Markita finished high school and got into college, her aunt said, she would pay for her college education. In return, after getting a job and starting a career, Markita would pay for the two of them to take a trip around the world together.

Markita found a way to flip that deal around. When she was 12 years old, there was a contest for selling Girl Scouts cookies. The winner who sold the most cookies for the year would be rewarded with an all-expenses-paid trip around the world for two.

When Markita knocked on doors, she didn't say, "Would you like to buy some Girl Scout cookies?" Instead, she started with her Why.

"Hi, my name s Markita Andrews. I'm a Girl Scout, and I want you to help me make my aunt's dream come true."

She won that contest — because she was marketing her mission.

Your Mission Helps Your Advocates Do Good Work

The product Markita was selling was incidental. It was an avenue for her customer to assist her in fulfilling her mission. When people buy into your mission, they don't mind paying a few dollars more or telling others about you. By bringing you more customers, they feel like they're also doing good work by supporting your mission.

When you're marketing your mission, you'll make more sales, with fewer objections — and improve the world by doing it.

What is your Why? Do your customers know it? Can they recite it? Would they support you more if you sold them your mission before selling them your stuff?

When you can clearly articulate your Why, you can sell that mission alongside your product or service. Your customers can make the world a better place by supporting your business.

When you are marketing yourself, your mission is a foundational place to start.

ACTION STEPS FOR ELEVATING YOUR PLATFORM

Complete the exercises in the Cornerstone Workbooks at MarketingYourselfBook.com/workbooks:

SCAN ME

1. Set yourself up in a calm and focused environment.

2. Review the questions in the Mission Messaging Workbook.

3. Answer the introspective questions to discover your mission.

4. Write a clear, concise paragraph you can use as your mission statement.

5. Read the paragraph aloud, edit, and update until it feels natural.

6. Gather feedback from trusted colleagues.

Chapter 3

Sharing Customer Stories

*The beating heart of marketing is not polished collateral
but deep customer insight.*

— Visakan Veerasamy

When Timothy Sykes hired Neil Patel to increase his website traffic, Neil did what he was hired to do. The number of visitors to Timothy's landing pages increased by 26%. But that wasn't the big win. What was really effective, Neil said, is that by using case studies in the emails he sent, Timothy's overall sales grew by 185%.

It wasn't the increased traffic to the landing page that drove the increase in sales; it was storytelling with case studies. The conversion ratio of the traffic increased by 70%, and this increased his client's profit by $1.2 million a year. The traffic wasn't any different, other than the volume; what changed was how that traffic was treated. By using case studies, Neil harnessed the power of storytelling.

Storytelling with a case study is a practical method to concisely package benefits and results. Did you notice how many statistics I slipped into the story above? By creating a story arc, I was able to provide you with lots of data and numbers, without overwhelming you.

Providing statistics validates the effectiveness of what you sell (especially for left-brained thinkers). But if you throw a collection of numbers and percentages at a prospective customer, it's easy for them to get overwhelmed and confused. We don't want statistics to obscure the main point; we want to support it.

Right-brained people prefer a short story to a spreadsheet. While you can convey highly complicated information in a spreadsheet, it also requires the skill of data interpretation. Not everyone can do that (or wants to do that). But we can all interpret stories.

A before-and-after story of your happy customers will enable your future customers to recognize themselves in the same story. A case study illustrates how a challenge was overcome and describes the practical and emotional obstacles faced along the way. By the end of a case study that's told as a good story, your future customer thinks, "That's what I want for my own story, too."

Here's a simple case study formula I use for Stellar Platforms:

1. Overview — introduction to the customer

2. Problem — the challenge they faced

3. Aim — how you planned to help

4. Obstacle — difficulty encountered along the way

5. Solution — how you solved it

6. Testimonial — how the customer felt

I don't have a brochure for my digital marketing agency. I direct them to the best sales page I've ever had, at stellarplatforms.com/case-studies. When someone is interested in hiring me for my marketing services, I send that link to demonstrate my credibility and to share powerful stories. Sharing the stories of happy customers with your future customers will bring you more customers than a slick brochure.

Case Studies Are Smart Marketing

According to a Hawkeye study, more than 70% of B2B buyers found testimonials and case studies to be the most influential types of content.1 If you want to persuade a customer to make a purchase, don't make a halfhearted post on social media. Pick up the phone and call a happy customer. Interview them about their experience with you and share that experience with your future customers.

"Asking the right questions in an interview will reveal your customer's story from start to finish — the pains that drove them, the factors that influenced their decision, and the results they've achieved," says Joel Klettke, the founder of Case Study Buddy.2 Joel has made it his business to articulate a great customer experience from the point of view of the customer.

Among B2B marketers, 65% rank case studies among their top three most effective types of content, and 62% of US agency executives claim that case studies are the most effective content for lead generation.3 We want people to feel empathy for the customers in our case studies. We want them to identify with their situation and think, "Hey, I'm like that." Then we want to illustrate the problems that customer faces. ("I face that problem, too!") Effective case studies illustrate how the challenge was overcome, describing the obstacles that were faced along the way.

1 Rachel Foster, "How to Use Case Studies to Drive B2B Sales," LinkedIn, last modified October 28, 2014, https://www.linkedin.com/pulse/20141028122751-36414330-how-to-use-case-studies-to-drive-b2b-sales/

2 Joel Klettke, "7 Great Sales & Marketing Insights You Can Get From One Customer Interview," Case Study Buddy, last modified August 16, 2016, https://casestudybuddy.com/tomer-interview/

3 "Agencies Use Content, Case Studies to Generate Leads: LinkedIn leads as best social network for recruiting new business," eMarketer, Insider Intelligence, last modified September 13, 2013, https://www.emarketer.com/Article/Agencies-Use-Content-Case-Studies-Generate-Leads/1010213

The Neuroscience of Storytelling

The five-act dramatic structure was defined by Gustav Freytag in 1863 to describe a story progression that is universal across cultures. Our brains are hard-wired for processing stories this way. For thousands of generations, our ancestors sat around the fire to share their favorite tales. The stories that lasted through the ages were the ones that followed a specific progression of emotions. This progression releases a series of hormones in our brains, and we've come to expect them in this order.

1. Oxytocin: the empathy hormone

2. Cortisol: the stress hormone

3. Endorphins: the euphoria hormones

4. Dopamine: the reward hormone

5. Serotonin: the balance hormone

If you skip a step in the five-act structure, your story will feel incomplete. People may stop listening if their brain expects an endorphin or dopamine hit that doesn't happen. By describing a series of events along this universal pattern, you're much more likely to keep your audience's attention.

Why are stories so effective? They reflect the emotions and language of your customers. Experts often can't see the problem clearly. As an expert, you're prone to use sophisticated language, but the specialized terms you use to discuss solutions don't generally resonate with your customers.

Nonexperts phrase their pain in beginner's language. You can gain access to this language if you ask your customers to describe their problems to you.

> *The key is to not try to tell the market anything.*
> *Celebrate the fact that the market will tell you.*
>
> — Jay Abraham

How Does Your Customer Say It?

A car mechanic doesn't use technical terms to diagnose what's wrong with your car. "What kind of a sound does it make?" and "What happens when you try to pump the gas?" are much clearer questions for the average driver to answer than "Is the fuel line clogged?" or "How much air is flowing through the carburetor?"

If you've ever seen a mechanic advertise on a billboard, you can see the kinds of beginner language that is effective in that industry. For an average driver, a picture of a scrunched-up car is a simple way to phrase your pain. You can understand what that means — the car is wrecked. But the billboard with the diagram of the clogged fuel line, using technical terms to describe the solution , is going to get ignored.

When you share stories and case studies describing the challenges of your customers, you resonate.

Resonation is a physics phenomenon that happens when an object is vibrating at a specific frequency, and other objects nearby are prone to vibrating at that frequency as well. Hold a tuning fork next to a wine glass and it will resonate with it, matching the vibrations in the air to make it sing.

To make sure your messaging is resonating with your customers, reflect your customers' own phrases back to them. Use the words they use to describe their current challenges, as well as the future outcome that they want.

41

RESONANT MESSAGING

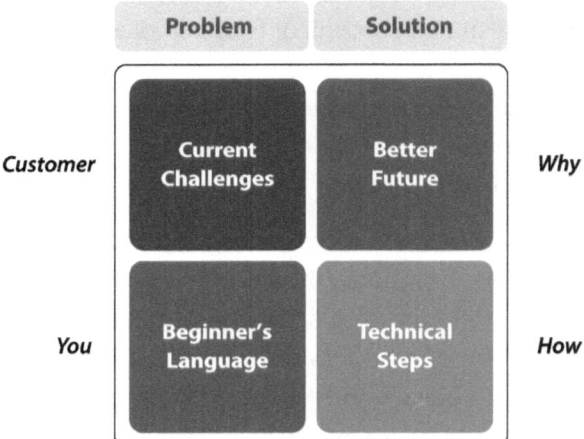

Ask Your Customers

Ryan Levesque describes the survey funnel he uses in his book, *Ask: The Counterintuitive Method to Discover Exactly What Your Customers Want to Buy.* His campaigns gathered more than 10,000 leads a day. He asked 2.8 million leads to fill out his survey and gained 175,000 customers across 19 different industries. When you review survey data, you'll often see a word or a phrase that turns up multiple times. Structuring headlines around the most common language a target market uses will make them think you're talking directly to them when they read your headlines.

> *Communicate with customers so they feel like*
> *you're talking TO them and not AT them.*
>
> — Ryan Levesque

Your ideas of what your customers want and how they would like to be sold are just that: ideas. Your ideas may be right or may be wrong.

Only testing will tell.

Take a shortcut to success by asking your customers what they really want with a survey. Then use the results to sell them what they say they want, instead of what you think they want.

If you don't have a survey in place, you can go to Google Forms or Typeform or Survey Monkey and make one in less than five minutes. Use the questions below, or edit them to better suit your market and your business:

- ✦ What's the biggest challenge you face with TOPIC?

- ✦ When was the last time that happened to you?

- ✦ Why was that so hard?

- ✦ What would make this easier?

- ✦ If a genie granted you a wish to solve this problem, what would change in your life and your business?

Set the answers to accept a full paragraph, and then share the form link with people in your target market. Copy and paste the invitation below from the Simple Survey Worksheet. Add your own content where words are in CAPS.

> *Hi, do you have a couple minutes to answer a short survey? I'm asking people like you about TOPIC, and I would love to hear your thoughts. This will only take a few minutes of your time, and I would really value your insight. LINK*

After you've collected plenty of responses (20–30 is a good starting goal, but the more the merrier), you can review the responses in bulk. Google Forms will automatically populate a spreadsheet with every answer laid out neatly for your review. (Pro tip: Add a checkbox at the end of the survey to offer subscription to your email newsletter. See an example at CaelanHuntress.com/Survey.) This kind of market research takes time, but it can enrich your business over the long term.

ACTION STEPS FOR ELEVATING YOUR PLATFORM

Complete the exercises in the Cornerstone Workbooks at MarketingYourselfBook.com/workbooks:

1. Make a copy of the Simple Survey Worksheet.

2. Edit the introduction paragraph so it sounds like you, in your voice.

3. Edit the questions to match what you want to ask in your survey.

4. Create a survey form.

5. Test the form.

6. Make a list of two to three dozen people to ask to take your survey.

7. Copy/paste your introduction paragraph into individual messages.

Chapter 4

Personal Brand vs. Business Brand

Branding is simply a convenient package for a business idea.

— Marty Neumeier

Originally, a brand declared ownership of property. It was a symbol that was seared onto the side of livestock, so anyone could look at the brand on the side of cattle and identify the owner of this particular animal. Over time, a brand has evolved to represent the identity of a company or business. Our experience of brands is a collection of impressions about a suite of products and services. For convenience, we refer to this suite under the umbrella of a brand name.

Which one is best for you — a personal brand or a business brand? While this is a very personal question, it's also a business question, and there's no single correct answer. Some say a personal brand is best, combining both together under your personal name. Others say a business brand should remain separate from your personal identity. They're both right sometimes.

An entrepreneur starts a business because they're good at something. There's a craft or a process or a specific type of work that they're good at doing, and they often like doing it. Running a business, though, is a whole different craft.

Marketing Yourself

In Michael Gerber's book, *The E-Myth*, he describes a baker who's great at baking.[1] She follows conventional advice and starts her own bakery. Soon she gets so wrapped up in running her business, she doesn't have time to bake. All of her energy and attention is spent learning how to manage people, handle payroll, set up insurance, and negotiate local ordinances and legislation. She's no longer a baker; she's an entrepreneur.

If your business has its own brand, you can sell it to someone else and go back to focusing on your craft. But if your business is all about you and your expertise, it's difficult to separate your business brand from your personal brand. Some people say you shouldn't.

In the book *The Thought Leaders Practice* by Matt Church, Peter Cook, and Scott Stein, the authors advise that for a specific type of work, you should use a personal brand with your personal name.[2] If you go to see a lawyer, for instance, you're paying for that person's expertise. They have their own name on the door, and it's not a business name. They can't sell their practice to somebody else. The business is based on a person's experience in their field. If your expertise is the foundation of your brand, they argue, it makes more sense to brand that expertise under your personal name.

No matter what kind of business you're in, there are three factors in any brand: you, your business, and your audience. If we look at these three factors in terms of your message, your offers, and your work, we can identify how to position each one.

---

1 Michael E. Gerber, "The E-myth Revisited: Why Most Small Businesses Don't Work and What to Do About It." Collins Business, 1995

2 Matt Church, Peter Cook, & Scott Stein, "The Thought Leaders Practice," Thought Leaders Publishing, 2012.

Personal Brand vs. Business Brand

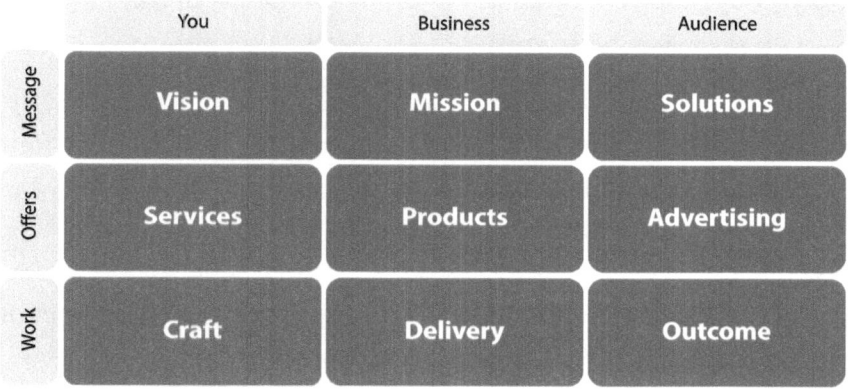

	You	Business	Audience
Message	Vision	Mission	Solutions
Offers	Services	Products	Advertising
Work	Craft	Delivery	Outcome

Most of your audience would be happy with the solution you deliver, whether it is through your personal brand or your business brand. So long as their problem gets solved, the name on the package is incidental. But what kind of relationship will they have with you, outside of the transaction? That's the question your brand can answer.

In some cases, having a business brand adjacent to your personal brand can work to your advantage.

Branding Case Study 1: Young Architect

Mike Riscica is the founder of YoungArchitect.com. His mission is to improve the next generation of architects. Mike has a very specific customer avatar: people studying for the National Council of Architectural Registration Board (NCARB) exam. They have a very specific buying trigger: graduating from architecture school. (We will cover buying triggers in chapter 12.) After completing their education and earning a diploma, young architects still have to spend months studying for their licensing exams. If you're already an architect or if you are still in architecture school, you're not his customer.

Right in between, directly after graduating from architecture school, you enter Mike's target demographic of young architects. You can join

Mike's study group to collaborate with a community of recent gradu-ates who study for the NCARB exam with you.

If Mike only used his own name as his brand, he would just be a tutor. A recent graduate from architecture school could work with this one guy who happens to help people with this specific kind of exam. But Mike doesn't want to tutor individuals; he wants to lead a movement. He wants to work with people who identify as Young Architects. His business brand calls them out by name. By using Young Architect as a separate brand, he has been able to create a community, and a conference, and a movement, and position himself as the leader.

Branding Case Study 2: The 25-Minute Meeting

Donna McGeorge is an Australian productivity expert and the author of *The 25-Minute Meeting*. People know her because of this remark-ably practical method for making meetings quick. There's a book and a website and a hashtag for this brand (#25MinuteMeeting), but nobody hires The 25-Minute Meeting for their organization. They hire Donna McGeorge.

This is an advantage of having a business brand. You can make the brand about the outcome, as Donna has done, or about the audience, as Mike does with Young Architect. Each of these could be considered a sidecar brand — a sub-brand attached to a personal brand, like a sidecar is attached to a motorcycle.

People can share the title of Donna's book, and instantly, they share the entire methodology and framework. But if you hire Donna to train your employees or speak at your conference, you don't hire The 25-Minute Meeting, you hire Donna.

Branding Case Study 3: Classical Guitar Shed

Allen Mathews is a guitar teacher who teaches in-person and virtual lessons one-on-one, but his website, ClassicalGuitarShed.com, doesn't rely on his personal name. Who goes online searching for a guy named Allen Mathews (2 Ls, one T) to take classical guitar lessons? Nobody. The unique spelling of his name makes him difficult to find, so what Allen does with his business brand is provide an easy way for strangers to find him.

Allen's website ranks for terms like "how to play classical guitar," which is easier because the words "classical guitar" are in his domain name. He writes long, detailed articles about how to play both basic and advanced pieces. After people engage with his business brand, they are then introduced to his personal brand, where they get to know him as a person. Allen introduces himself with a separate business brand because it makes it easier for him to attract strangers to his work.

Branding Case Study 4: Stellar Platforms

I think about living with complementary brands because I always struggle with my own branding. I have a business brand for my digital marketing agency, Stellar Platforms, where I help experts and entrepreneurs set up smart marketing systems. But in addition to digital marketing, I also create a lot of content about digital meetings and digital money, about balancing life and play. I pursue many different interests, and having a separate business brand allows me to be clear about things I produce professionally or personally.

If someone hires me to redesign their website because they know me personally, I still send an invoice on the Stellar Platforms letterhead. They're a client of my business, but the person that they hire is me. Even if I outsource the design of the website to a contractor, it makes sense that I'm using Stellar Platforms as the brand. My business finds and onboards the customers and manages the contractors to produce the work. In this instance, having two separate brands works well.

The author of this book, however, is not Stellar Platforms. I can grow the brand equity of Caelan Huntress while promoting my business at the same time. But this dilutes my effectiveness. When I produce a piece of content, I have to pause and consider which brand is the best for publishing.

After 10 years of relying on a business brand, what I've learned from leaning more into my personal brand is this: I still don't think of Stellar Platforms as a separate brand from mine (right now). But if I wanted, I could sell that agency to someone else, and the brand equity would be part of what they purchase.

This might be the biggest difference between a personal brand and a business brand: portable brand equity. You can sell a business brand to someone else, but with a personal brand, you can't.

Let's compare:

Business Brand Advantages:

- ✦ You can sell a business brand and exit the company.
- ✦ You can outsource the work to others.
- ✦ You have an intermediary entity for liability.

Business Brand Disadvantages:

- ✦ You have a lower level of trust from your audience.
- ✦ There's higher churn, meaning it's more likely that customers will go to competitors.
- ✦ It's harder to build an audience and stand out from the crowd.

Personal Brand Advantages:

- ✦ You accumulate brand equity no matter what you work on.
- ✦ If you pivot to a different venture, you take your audience with you.
- ✦ Sharing your personal life and quirks becomes business marketing.

Personal Brand vs. Business Brand

Personal Brand Disadvantages:

- ✦ Your presence and time are always required, since you cannot outsource yourself.

- ✦ If you stop working or producing, your brand loses value.

- ✦ Pivots to different projects and offers can confuse your audience.

Here's what it boils down to: your personality is a part of your branding.

Keep your business brand separate from your personal brand only if your business can be separated from you.

If your business can deliver or operate without you, keeping your business brand separate is a legitimate option. You'll be able to sell your business, and someone else can continue it without you. But the downside is you forfeit the brand equity in your personal name.

If you migrate from business to business and venture to venture, over time, a personal brand comes with you, while a business brand stops at the pivot. Keeping a single brand as your personal name protects your earned reputation for all time.

No matter what you accomplish, your personal brand accumulates reputation, trust, and authority, even as you pivot into new ventures.

If you have both a personal and a business brand, be intentional with what each brand shares. Studies have shown that when identical messages are shared on personal social media accounts instead of business brand accounts, they are shared an average of 24 times more often. So, if Pringles wants to share a branded message, it's 24 times more likely that it will be re-shared if a Pringles employee shares it personally rather than if the Pringles account shares it.

This is because people trust people, but distrust businesses. According to research conducted by Nielsen, when making a purchase decision, up to 92% of buyers are more likely to talk with a salesperson who also has their own personal brand.3 When a business has a discount promotion, it's not a big deal. But when a friend you know has a sale, the additional factor of friendship could sway your buying decision.

Personal Brand Basics

The first (and easiest) step to building your personal brand is setting up your personal email address. An example is "yourfirstname@your-fullname.com" which is an eponymous email address. People can reach you, at your website, about yourself. Even if you don't have a website, just setting up an eponymous email address is a cornerstone of your personal branding — "yourfullname@gmail.com" without any cute handles or identifiers is an email that belongs to someone with a personal brand.

Claiming social media handles for your full name is a good second step. If you can't get your exact name, close approximations with prefixes or suffixes work, too.

@therealCaleanHuntress or @CaelanHuntressinc or @mrCaelanHunt-ress are examples of personal brand handles that can be used when some other jerk with your name claims them first. (I'm looking at you, the guy who bought Caelan.com and did nothing with it.)

The third step is to make a logo with your name. You can pick a font (Google Fonts has plenty to choose from), put one of your names in bold and change the color, and save the screenshot as an image.

3 "Consumer Trust in Online, Social and Mobile Advertising Grows," Insights, Nielsen, last modified April 11, 2012, https://www.nielsen.com/us/en/insights/article/2012/consumer-trust-in-online-social-and-mobile-advertising-grows/.

This is how the logo I currently use on my personal website at CaelanHuntress.com was made, and it took five minutes to design.

Brands That Matter

In his book *The Brand Gap*, communication designer Marty Neumeier says a brand should answer three questions:

◆ Who are you?

◆ What do you do?

◆ Why does it matter?

Sharing yourself, your work, and why it matters is the simplest and clearest way to market yourself as a personal brand. If you post regularly about what you do, how you change the world, how the lives of your customers have been improved, and how you relate to your work, people will identify your personal brand as the expert on the topics you discuss.

Many entrepreneurs hesitate to share their personal lives for fear of putting off potential customers, but it's often the alignment of values and personality that actually endears us to brands and influences our buying decisions. That alignment is achieved when your audience resonates with your personal stories.

ACTION STEPS FOR ELEVATING YOUR PLATFORM

Complete the exercises in the Cornerstone Workbooks at MarketingYourselfBook.com/workbooks:

SCAN ME

1. Download the Personal Branding Checklist.

2. For every item in the Beginner list that you have completed, award yourself one point.

3. For every item in the Intermediate list that you have completed, award yourself two points.

4. For every item in the Advanced list that you have completed, award yourself three points.

5. Share your Personal Branding Score on social media with the hashtag #MarketingYourselfBook.

6. Identify which outstanding items you want to accomplish this week, this month, and this year.

7. Schedule time in your calendar to accomplish those things.

Cornerstone 2

Profit

*Minimum viable income is a point of stasis when
your runway becomes infinite.*

— Corbett Barr

Profit is the difference between the value you put into something and the value you get out of it. To have a profitable platform, your output of money (or status or energy) has to be greater than your input. The easiest way to calculate the profit of a platform is financial: are you making enough revenue to stay on your platform?

Money isn't the only metric that matters in a business — it just happens to be the simplest to measure. You can quantify your success through your sales, no matter what you do in your business. Whether you're a self-employed freelancer, an enterprise company, or a non-profit organization, you're selling one of three things:

✦ a product

✦ a service

✦ a mission

Alone, a product or a service can change an experience for your customer. But if you combine your service with a mission, you change lives. If you combine a product with a mission, you change the world.

Why is it, then, that selling this change can feel so difficult and fake?

Selling is the mechanism through which you provide value to the world. When people buy what you're selling, this enables you to continue contributing that value. It's an acknowledgment of worthiness, a trade that benefits everyone. Why should this reciprocation of value feel sleazy?

Selling feels sleazy when you confuse the difference between sales and marketing. Learning when to push and when to pull removes a lot of the friction from growing your business.

In this section, you're going to learn about how to generate profit from your platform. This will include financial profit, but also the profit of reputation, satisfaction, and relationships.

Chapter 5

The 4-Step Marketing Cycle

All things being equal, people will do business with,
and refer business to, those people they know, like, and trust.

— Bob Burg

As a teenager, I first learned the effectiveness of marketing yourself when I was selling doughnuts door-to-door. Every Saturday morning for three months, as a fundraiser for my high school drama club, I would knock on the doors of strangers, introduce myself, and make my pitch to sell a dozen doughnuts. Within a few minutes, the stranger either handed me five bucks or shut the door in my face. Every sale was a struggle — until I learned about the 4-Step Marketing Cycle.

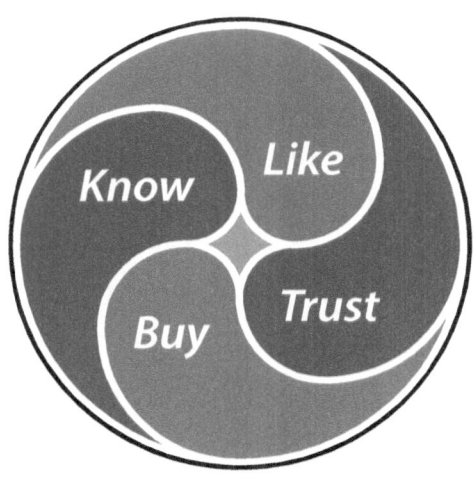

Marketing Yourself

One Saturday morning, I tried an experiment. I bought two dozen doughnuts myself and gave one to every house on Johnson Street. "Here's a free doughnut," I said after I introduced myself. "I'll be back next weekend, and ask you to buy a dozen to support our fundraiser. See you then!"

The next Saturday, I made more sales on Johnson Street than all the other streets combined. Instead of selling to strangers, I invested time (and earned trust) by following the 4-Step Marketing Cycle: Know, Like, Trust, and Buy.

Each step in this cycle is a deepening of your relationship with someone. If you try to skip a step, you can lose the sale, damage your relationship, or scare people away for good.

Selling doughnuts to strangers, I was surprised to find that by creating a simple relationship, I was able to dramatically increase my success by saying: — 1. Hello, 2. Here's a free sample, 3. This is my promise, 4. I'll fulfill that promise. My success didn't come from knocking on more doors, changing my prices, or refusing to take no for an answer; it was the result of creating more relationships.

Marketing yourself to strangers who could become customers is similar to feeding a timid wild animal. You have to be patient. Move slowly. Get them to like what you're offering from a safe distance. You can be delicate about how you deliver your gift, or you can throw food at them (right before they run away). Even though your intention is to be helpful, you can't move at your own speed. Until trust has been built up over time, you need to move at a slower speed that makes strangers feel comfortable with you.

If you don't know someone who's selling to you, or you don't like their personality, or you don't trust what they say, you won't feel confident in buying from them. You need to take enough time in all four steps in the marketing cycle to make it smoothly to the sale.

The 4-Step Marketing Cycle

Guiding people through this four-step progression is how strangers become customers. If they know you, but only a little bit, you can increase their knowledge of you before moving them to the next step in the cycle. Make someone a fan before you try to earn their trust. Enroll people in advocating for you before asking them to buy from you.

By raising the intensity from low to high in their current stage of the 4-Step Marketing Cycle, you'll make it easier for them to move into the next stage.

1. Know — Turn a Stranger Into a Lead

To become known, talk openly about your areas of expertise. Be generous with your knowledge. Staying on brand and on message will help people to understand you. If people can categorize you easily, they'll come to you first when they face the problems you solve.

Find communities where your customers already congregate. Go there, offer your expertise, and talk about why instead of how. When people don't know you, giving them a whole lot of instruction isn't going to grab their attention. If you talk about why something is important, you'll get a lot more people who offer to pay you for the how.

To get known, answer questions like:

- ✦ What do you do?
- ✦ What are you like?
- ✦ Why should I care?

2. Like — Turn the Indifferent Into Fans

Some people are well-known and yet not well-liked. Talking with many people is useful, but relationships are built individually. When talking with your customers, find a way to engage with individuals one-on-one. It takes time when you start, but that affection can turn into advocacy, if you can make a direct improvement on someone's life.

For the last 10–20 years, anybody with a business has put together a website and an email newsletter list. But that doesn't mean they use them well. Blasting your message one way isn't enough to build a relationship. You need to balance authenticity with automation to turn indifferent people into fans.

To get liked, answer questions like:

✦ Do you care about me?

✦ Will I regret spending time with you?

✦ Do you make my life better?

3. Trust — Turn the Suspicious Into Advocates

Only 3% of B2B buyers say they trust someone with the title "sales representative," but 79% said they would buy from a "trusted adviser."[1] People know a selling relationship isn't genuine because every salesperson has an agenda: they want to part you from your money.

As you market yourself, don't be your own sales representative. Become a trusted adviser for your customer by being someone who adds value to their life. Developing a trust-based relationship involves more than a transaction. It starts with your investment — an investment of your time, curiosity, and commitments.

To get trusted, answer questions like:

✦ Will you do what you say you'll do?

✦ What's your real agenda?

✦ Can I believe you?

---

1 Aja Frost, "Only 3% of People Think Salespeople Possess This Crucial Character Trait," Blogs, HubSpot, last modified July 28, 2017, https://blog.hubspot.com/sales/salespeople-perception-problem

4. Buy — Turning a Prospect Into a Customer

A selling conversation is very different from a marketing conversation. Marketing yourself invites the right people to come to you and say, "Hey, I know you, I like you, I trust you, and I want to buy what you have to sell." Guiding people through the 4-Step Marketing Cycle means you don't have to be your own salesperson. You can be a trusted advisor, someone who handles incoming leads, instead of going out to convince strangers to buy what they're selling.

To sell your product or service, answer questions like:

✦ How much will this cost?

✦ What will I get?

✦ What else do I need to know?

THE BUYER'S MATRIX

	Know	Like	Trust	Buy
High	Lead	Fan	Advocate	Customer
Medium	Aware	Interested	Skeptical	Suspect
Low	Stranger	Indifferent	Suspicious	Prospect

The best thing about the 4-Step Marketing Cycle is that at the end of the cycle, it starts over again — but you get to the Buy step much more quickly with people who already Know, Like, and Trust you. According to Forrester Research, it takes five times more money to acquire a new customer than it does to sell to an existing one.2 In fact, 61% of small-to-medium-sized businesses report that less than half of their revenue comes from new business; a majority of SMB revenue comes from repeat customers.

When you're planning to elevate your message and grow your audience, don't overlook the biggest fans that are already right next to your platform. They take less convincing, and they're statistically more likely to buy from you than anyone else.

Kevin Kelley, the founding editor of *Wired* magazine, famously talked about how 1,000 true fans are enough to sustain a lifestyle business. He said that 1,000 true fans who will buy what you're selling are all you need to create your own business and make a good living from that audience. Millions of people have done this, all over the world, from every kind of background and situation.

And it works because the 4-Step Marketing Cycle is continuous. If you're generous with what you know, you engage with individuals one-on-one, and you ask good questions that demonstrate you understand their challenges, people will Know you, Like you, Trust you, and — ultimately — Buy from you.

---

2 Alan E. Webber and E. G. Brown, "B2B Customer Experience Priorities In an Economic Downturn: Key Customer Usability Initiatives In A Soft Economy," Forrester Research, Inc., February 19, 2008, https://www.forrester.com/report/B2B-Customer-Experience-Priorities-In-An-Economic-Downturn/RES41225

ACTION STEPS FOR ELEVATING YOUR PLATFORM

Complete the exercises in the Cornerstone Workbooks at MarketingYourselfBook.com/workbooks:

SCAN ME

1. Make a copy of the template Marketing Cycle Trello Board.

2. Read the instructions on the first card.

3. List the people in your network who belong on all four lists.

4. Identify a specific action to move people from one list to the next.

5. Schedule time on your calendar to work this board, when you'll encourage people to take those actions. It's great if you can make movement on it daily, but make the commitment to at least look at it each day.

Chapter 6

Pushing vs. Pulling

To market something is to make it beautiful in the right way.

— Venkatesh Rao

Selling is where you want to go. Marketing is why you want to get there.

In the split-second you see a hitchhiker on the side of the road, you make an instant decision whether to pull over or not. That immediate reaction is the difference between success and failure to a hitchhiker. Selling and marketing will give you very different results.

In a classic pair of photos by advertising executive Alex Bogusky, he showed the same hitchhiker holding two different signs that created very different reactions. The first sign said "Jacksonville." The second sign said "Mom's for Christmas."

The first sign tells you where the hitchhiker is going. If you happen to be going to Jacksonville, there's alignment — but it's still up to you to decide whether you want to pick him up.

The second sign tells you his mission, why he's hitchhiking. The destination might not actually factor into your decision. You could be going somewhere else entirely and decide to pick him up anyway because you support his mission. If you focus on where before why, you may not persuade anyone to pick you up.

Marketing Is Selling at Scale

Before I got into marketing, I was in sales for a few years. The psychology and science of selling were fascinating to me, and I'm glad I learned them. The difference between the two disciplines is that selling convinces one person to buy right now, while marketing convinces many people to buy over time. The open-ended timeline of marketing is slower than sales. You're developing a relationship to influence a buying decision. You offer periodic calls to action, and that converts some people into customers.

With selling, you focus on the individual prospect right in front of you. This encourages psychological manipulation tactics, because they are effective one-on-one. Selling is biased toward the now, while marketing is biased toward the future.

Marketing expert Seth Godin likes to say that an interruption marketer is a hunter, while a permission marketer is a farmer. Hunters go find fresh meat, while farmers grow food slowly. This difference is well-known in sales communities. Some salespeople are hunters who go and seek out new deals. Others are farmers who nurture relationships that eventually grow into deals. Marketing is like farming leads, and selling is like hunting leads. Anyone can shepherd a customer through their journey. You just need to know when to push, and when to pull — when to be a farmer, and when to be a hunter.

Moving From Marketing to Sales

If you draw three concentric circles, you can place your customers in the center circle. Those are the people who earn your service. You don't give service to people you're still selling to; prospective customers go in the second circle. You treat people in the second circle differently than the customers in the first. Your conversations with these people will be focused on getting them into the inner circle of your customers, crossing the boundary where they make a purchase.

If you treat these people in the second circle like customers and help them solve problems before they've paid you, they may find no incentive to become your customer. It's only once someone has paid you that they become a customer.

MARKETING IS PULLING, SALES IS PUSHING

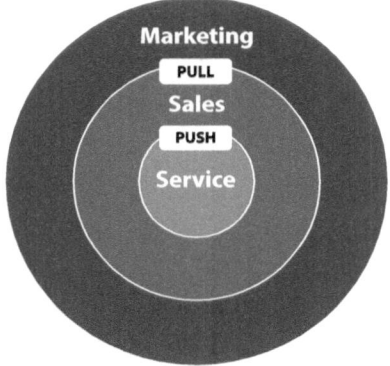

Before payment, they're not. There's a very clear dividing line between these two circles: the financial transaction.

There's a similar dividing line between marketing and sales. When someone is in the outermost circle, marketing to them is fine, but selling to them can feel pushy.

Selling Only Feels Pushy If You Haven't Done Enough Pulling

Marketing is what happens on the outside of a shop window. Shopkeepers entice window shoppers to come inside by setting up a nice storefront, posting big signs, and offering incentives to voluntarily enter the store. If it's appealing from the outside, you'll go in.

Once you cross the threshold, it's fair game for a shopkeeper to sell to you. If you pick an item up off a shelf, and a clerk comes up to you to ask, "Would you like to purchase that?" it's not pushy at all. You're in their store, looking at an item, and considering whether you want to buy it. Selling is fair game, inside the shop.

But it's not the right time to start selling to someone when they're still outside the shop, before they've decided to go inside. The work of marketing yourself is to pull people closer to you and to get them to voluntarily take the step that signals they're ready for sales.

The transition from marketing into sales is voluntary, and you can't do it for them. It happens when they no longer need to be convinced of your value. They Know, Like, and Trust you, and then they want to know the specifics of how they can engage you commercially. This boundary is crossed when the customer volunteers a willingness to enter the sales conversation. If you try selling to them before they take that voluntary step, it might backfire, and they might be repulsed by your efforts.

Prospective Customers Volunteer To Be Sold

For my digital marketing agency, Stellar Platforms, the transition from marketing to sales happens when someone requests a marketing consultation. I market to my audience by talking about the problems I solve and telling stories of people who've seen these results change their life or their business. While I don't directly say, "Hire me to do this for you, too," I mention my offers in the context of my work. I don't sell directly to my audience at large. I only sell to people who raise their hand and say, "I'd like your advice on my business."

After someone has voluntarily crossed the first boundary, filled out a consultation application, and scheduled an appointment, then I spend some time brainstorming with them. I learn about their business, provide value, and if it seems like a good fit, I make an offer to work together. At that point, I can use my selling skills to sell that offer. But if I try that too early, I'll scare them off.

Pushing vs. Pulling

If I tried to sell my services before people asked for information about a possible transaction, before they voluntarily crossed from marketing to sales, then selling would feel sleazy. But when you pull people to you through marketing, selling is just a natural push.

Pull Before You Push

Identify when a customer moves from your marketing circle into the sales circle. What is the specific step when someone signals they're ready to have a sales conversation?

In the world of digital marketing, sometimes we convert cold traffic into customers on a single sales page. We do this by starting with marketing on the top of the page, pulling them further and further down, until we make a push at the end. There is a 21-step sales letter formula developed by Perry Belcher that pulls people in at the top of the page and pushes them to buy at the bottom.[1]

1. Call out to your audience

2. Get their attention

3. Back up the big promise headline with a quick explanation

4. Identify the problem

5. Provide the solution

6. Show pain of and cost of development

7. Explain ease-of-use

8. Show speed to results

9. Future cast

10. Show your credentials

11. Detail the benefits

12. Get social proof

---

1   *Perry Belcher, "Salesletter Formula," https://perrybelcher.com /21-step-salesletter-formula/*

13. Make your offer

14. Add bonuses

15. Build up your value

16. Reveal your price

17. Inject scarcity

18. Give guarantee

19. Call to action

20. Give a warning

21. Close with a reminder

Do you notice how the first 12 steps are all pulling, and there isn't any pushing until the end?

If you don't want to be pushy, don't use your marketing to sell.

Use your marketing to pull, and only push when prospects volunteer that they're ready. Unlike on a sales page, your sales process might have an action between marketing and sales — filling out a form, requesting a quote, or calling you on the phone.

Focus your marketing on encouraging the one action that makes customers ready to have a sales conversation.

ACTION STEPS FOR ELEVATING YOUR PLATFORM

Complete the exercises in the Cornerstone Workbooks at MarketingYourselfBook.com/workbooks:

SCAN ME

1. Make a copy of the Sales Letter Formula Workbook.

2. Write a sentence or a paragraph under each heading. Notice how everything from 1 through 12 is marketing and 13 through 21 is sales.

3. Use the language from 1 to 12 in your marketing materials.

4. If you find any topics from 13 to 21 in your marketing, consider moving them after your prospect has made a voluntary request.

5. Share your sales page with the hashtag **#MarketingYourselfBook** to ask for some feedback — and get a signal boost!

Chapter 7

Free Samples Whet the Appetite

To build trust, you must create value and safety
for the person you want to influence.

— Melanie Marshall

Without trust, you can't complete the 4-Step Marketing Cycle, and letting customers try you before they buy you is the best way to build trust. Free samples are a shortcut.

Would you want to take a car for a test drive before purchasing it? Of course you would. Whether you're buying a new car from a dealer or a used car from the previous owner, taking a test drive is a basic method to learn about the car you're thinking of buying. Without a test drive, you don't have enough information (or experience) to make a purchase.

If you've ever bought or sold a used car from an individual, you know the importance of trust in the sales process. Chances are, neither of you is an expert in automobiles. When both of the people in a used car transaction are amateurs, they'll each feel a little anxious and vulnerable. The exchange only happens when the time is right, the trust is right, and the money is right.

To get to that point of equilibrium between value and safety, the seller offers a free sample of driving the car. They know that getting you into the driver's seat is necessary to get you to buy it. Imagine how you'd feel, getting into a car to take it on a test drive, and the seller says, "It's five dollars for the gas."

Would you pay for the test drive? Or would you leave right then? A seller this stingy, charging you for gas to go around the block, might not make a fair deal with you. Because you both are amateurs, trust is important. If you think the other person might be shifty or dishonest, would you want to spend thousands of dollars on a deal with them?

If the price were low enough, you might decide the purchase is worth the risk. Conversely, if the trust is high enough, you might be willing to pay top dollar. These are the two factors that are necessary to make a purchase happen: trust and money.

- ✦ When there's high trust and a high price, you can sell.
- ✦ When there's low trust and a low price, you can sell.
- ✦ It's nearly impossible to sell a high-priced item with low trust.
- ✦ The surest way to sell is with high trust and a low price.

TRUST VS COST

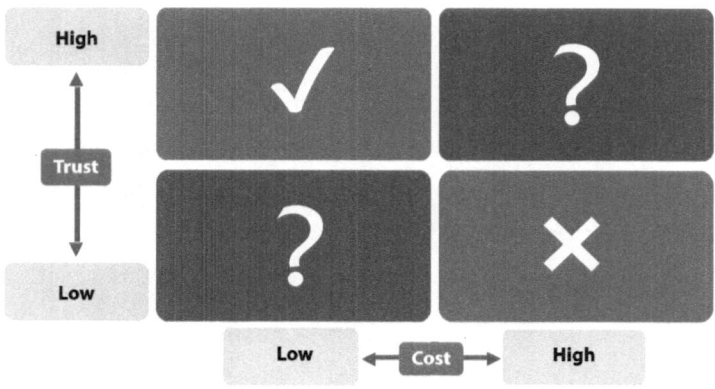

If you're selling services, time, or expertise, a free consultation is an easy way to be generous and build trust with your target market. The only thing your customer invests is time. Before you convince someone to spend money with you, convince them to spend time with you, so they can give you a test drive.

Prime the Pump

When you drill a well into the ground to draw water up out of the earth, the pump won't work if it's completely dry. You have to add some water to the pump at the top, before it can pull more water up from down below. This is known as "priming the pump," and the concept applies to other scenarios, as well. If you want to start a fire with a pile of wood, you have to bring a little bit of fire to get things started. In other words, supplying a little bit of what you want is how you create the conditions to bring in more.

If you want to do business with someone, a free consultation primes the pump. They receive some value from you, which makes them more willing to give value back to you (in the form of cash). They also gain a clear understanding of what they can achieve by working with you in the future. A whopping 96% of buyers think a meeting is worth their time if you focus on the value you deliver to them. A free consultation is a low-risk method to demonstrate your value to a potential customer.

Case Study 1: Big Idea Brainstorms

When I first started traveling as a digital nomad, I supported my young family by running a website design agency. When we moved to Costa Rica, I called my business Pura Vida MultiMedia, an homage to the national slogan of that country. I earned most of my clients through giving free consultations over video calls. I called these sessions "Big Idea Brainstorms," because I liked working with people who were starting their first business (and needed a website for it).

My free sample focused on helping entrepreneurial people brainstorm their big idea. For years, I would talk to anybody. If you had an idea for a business, and you were willing to fill out an application form telling me about your idea, I'd get on a call with you for half an hour and offer some free advice.

Statistically, 30% of those free consultations turned into my customers. By tracking my numbers, I was able to monitor how many free consultations I gave and how many clients I earned from that activity. This helped me anticipate what to expect from my lead generation. If I scheduled three consultations in a week, I could expect, on average, one new client that week.

Free consultations are effective because they can give you intelligence you can use to close the sale. Asking detailed questions about specific needs, priorities, and challenges will give you valuable insight. You can position your solution as the way they can achieve the outcome that they specifically said they want. All you have to do is discover the details.

Over time, free samples may become the front end of your business. Anywhere you go, you can offer a free sample, and the right kinds of people will be interested. Offer free value, build trust, make an offer. When a customer's buying decision depends on you, your personality, and your trustworthiness, offering a free sample to the right target market could become your most lucrative marketing activity.

Case Study 2: Book Talk Tuesdays

Erin Donley offers a free consultation she calls Book Talk Tuesdays. She's a ghostwriter who helps people who have stories to tell, and her personal statement is, "I work with industry experts who want to clarify their message, rise above the noise, and finish the books they've been wanting to write." Her calendar is open every Tuesday for any first-time author who have a book in them.

If you've dreamed of writing a book, you can schedule 30 minutes with Erin to talk about any aspect of nonfiction book creation, whether or not you want to hire a ghostwriter. She can explain how to get started, how to choose or clarify your topic, and how to develop chapters. Since she managed a bookstore for many years, people contact Erin just to see if their idea is both viable and relevant.

Not every consultation turns into a client for her ghostwriting practice, but all of them turn into advocates. Every consultation who doesn't hire Erin is another weak tie in her network. Remember the weak ties from chapter 1? Anytime a weak tie hears that someone is struggling with finishing their book, that person can say, "I know a ghostwriter. Would you like me to make an introduction?"

Providing value for free and regularly creating trust with people can build a network that supports your career. This is a longer game of marketing yourself than pay-per-click ads or five-day funnels, but the short game has to be restored and refilled all the time. If you want stability and longevity in your business, play the long game.

Earning Trust for Free

When courting a new customer, the highest barrier to overcome is trust. Trust can be earned through generosity, and a low price is an effective way to be generous. The lowest-priced offer you can make is free. Ironically, customers do not think something free is of low value.

In 2007, a study by MIT found that people think a zero-dollar price adds to the benefits of a product.[1] The "last benefit difference" is psychologically different for zero dollars. It turns out, people assume that if you put in the effort to make something for free, that means it

---

1   Dan Ariely and Kristina Shampan'er, "Zero as a special price: The true value of free products," Marketing Science 26, no. 6 (2007): 742-757, https://web.mit.edu/ariely/www/MIT/Papers/zero.pdf

must be good. At the very least, it should be good enough to justify the time they take to consume it.

Offering a free sample lowers a customer's risk, demonstrates what they would get from you, and gives them an incentive to start working with you before money changes hands. With the right strategy, offering free consultations can become your primary method of lead generation.

Here's how you can set up a simple free consultation system:

1. **Create an intake form.** Some typical methods that people use as of this writing include Google Forms, Typeform, or Survey Monkey.

2. **List questions.** Ask questions in your form that will help you come to the conversation prepared with ideas. (For inspiration, you can see my intake form at StellarPlatforms.com/Consultation.)

3. **Automate delivery.** Have form submissions sent directly to your email inbox or your customer relationship management program. Test this yourself a time or two with dummy accounts. Make sure the emails arrive to you and to the prospective customer the way you'd like.

4. **Set up a scheduling tool.** Calendly, Schedule Once, and Acuity are programs that allow you to select an appointment from available times on your calendar. You can have as many (or as few) open slots as you choose.

5. **Automate delivery of your scheduling link.** After someone submits an intake form, they should receive the link to schedule an appointment with you on the very next page. It's best if the scheduling system sends reminder emails, too, so all you have to do is show up.

6. **Write your pitch.** What is the specific wording you will use to offer someone a free consultation? Work on this paragraph until it's seamless, so you can recite it or paste it with minimal effort.

Here's a brief example:

"I'd like to talk with you about growing your business. If you'd like a free, no-obligation consultation, fill out this form, and we can schedule a time to connect."

When you're giving a free consultation, remember to focus on why, and not how. It's easy to fall into discussing how you can fix their problems, but you're more likely to close the deal if you focus on why they want their problems fixed during this free consultation.

I know it sounds counterintuitive, but what a new customer wants most from you isn't an understanding of how they can fix their problem themselves ... they want to know why you're the right person to do it for them.

The reason this shift worked so well for me was that I often consulted myself out of a sale by offering too much free value. I'd get so excited about working with the new customer, I'd tell them during our call how they could do it themselves.

You don't want to feed someone free samples until they're full, if what you want is for them to make a purchase that sates their hunger.

ACTION STEPS FOR ELEVATING YOUR PLATFORM

Complete the exercises in the Cornerstone Workbooks at MarketingYourselfBook.com/workbooks:

SCAN ME

1. Download the Free Consultation Worksheet, which has some of my best questions to ask during a free consultation.

2. Read all the questions out loud. Rewrite any questions that would sound more natural to you if they were worded differently.

3. Role-play a free consultation with a friendly colleague and ask them for feedback on the conversation.

4. Schedule a conversation with a live prospect for a free consultation and record the call.

5. Review the recording, making notes on how you can improve your consultation.

6. Write your pitch. What is the specific wording you will use to offer a free consultation? Work on this paragraph until it's seamless, so you can recite it or paste it with minimal effort.

Chapter 8

Calling to Action

A decision is made with the brain. A commitment is made with the heart.
Therefore, a commitment is much deeper and more binding
than a decision.

— Dr. Nido Qubein

I received a party invitation and a sales pitch on the same day. One made me uncomfortable, and the other did not.

The sales pitch took place on a used car lot. I happened to be walking by, and on a whim, I wandered in to look at some prices. Smelling a potential customer, a salesperson came over and quoted me a price. When I shrugged, he used all sorts of sleazy sales tactics. This was my only shot at getting a deal like this, he said. He belittled the car I currently drove and hounded me about my budget.

I left and went to the post office, where I found a party invitation in the mail. I didn't want to go, and I didn't need to tell anyone. There was an RSVP envelope included with the invitation that I held on to until later in the week. By the time I took out the invitation to check one of the boxes, I'd changed my mind, and I'd decided to attend.

Combining the buying decision with the call to action (CTA) is what makes selling sleazy. When I received the party invitation in the mail, that was a call to action. In the near future, I had to make a decision.

I would attend the party, decline the invitation, or ignore it and not respond.

My buying decision didn't happen when I opened the envelope. Opening the envelope was only the call to action.

Because I had time and space to make a decision, I didn't feel like the person inviting me was being pushy or gross. But if they'd called me on the phone to ask immediately, "I'm having a party on Friday, will you come?" this would have combined the CTA with the decision. If I wanted to say no, I would have felt pushed into making a decision right there on the phone. Pressuring me to make a decision is what the car salesman was trying to do by combining the buying decision with the call to action.

A call to action is only an invitation.

The CTA does not need to convince or persuade. Its only purpose is to articulate the next step.

The car salesman could have separated the CTA from the buying decision by saying, "My office is through that door. If you want to discuss pricing, come right on in. I'll make you a cup of coffee." The sleazy feeling of sales pressure would have been removed. I would have been given an opportunity to make a microcommitment to voluntarily signal my interest. The low-stakes enticement — free coffee — would have smoothed any resistance I felt and kept our communication comfortable.

By practicing a simple and clear call to action, you can easily transition conversations about hypotheticals into commercial engagements.

Nine-Word Email CTA

In email marketing, there's a useful tactic called a "nine-word email." This email is sent to a segment of your list that once expressed interest.

Calling to Action

I have a segment of my newsletter list called "Coaching Interest." This small sublist of people have expressed interest in my coaching programs. They may have applied for a free consultation or clicked through to read my coaching page in the past.

When I want some money, I send a nine-word email to this segment of my list. Something like, "Are you interested in hiring me as your coach?" I don't need to persuade this segment. I know they're interested. They know enough to already know the basics of my pitch. I could add testimonials on top of the CTA or overwhelm my message with lots of features and benefits. But that would combine the buying decision with the call to action and make my message muddy.

Instead, I just ask a simple question: "Is now the right time?" If so, they reply. If not, they ignore the message and move on with their life. A simple, clear CTA is a non-threatening invitation you can give out to anyone who might be interested in buying from you. But an invitation alone is not enough to convince people that they should act.

The Struggle Between the Heart and the Head

On the third day we were stranded in the airport, I began to make bad decisions. The kids were hungry — again. The healthy snacks my wife prepared had run out the day before. The food choices near the departure gate looked appetizing, despite the behavior problems that we knew prepackaged foods cause in the sensitive stomachs of our children.

Traveling for five days with my wife and three young kids, we were bumped from two consecutive flights. There were still two more days of travel ahead of us until we finally made it to New Zealand. LAX is not the best of airports, and my resilience was fading.

We could have left the airport and taken a taxi to a health food store, to prepare wholesome, nutritious, and bland meals for everyone. This would have taken hours and cost a bunch of money, and we would have had to go through security again. Or, we could just buy them tasty, convenient sandwiches.

My head said: make the extra effort, spend the extra money, do what's right.
My heart said: buy the cheap food now, it's too much effort to do this right.

This struggle, between our heads and our hearts, is how we make a Buying Decision. Understanding this struggle — and talking to both the head and the heart — is the key to convincing someone to buy from you.

Emotions and Logic Are Often at Odds

It's almost like you have two different personalities on your internal decision-making committee: the Junkie and the Janitor. The Junkie is your quick-fix, do-it-now, impulsive heart. The Janitor is the one who is cautious about making messes that have to be cleaned up later.

What your inner Junkie wants is often different than what your inner Janitor wants. My inner Janitor was worried about the behavior of my kids on the long plane ride across the Pacific, later. My inner Junkie wanted to fix the hangry behavior of my kids at the airport, right then.

When emotion and logic are at odds in a purchasing decision, emotion often wins. So when you want to convince someone to make a decision, speak to the heart and not to the head.

Would You Like To Solve This Problem?

The brain processes emotion and reason very differently. Even if you can't logically justify a decision, you sometimes go against your logic because of a gut feeling. We have nonrational senses that signal when an illogical decision is still the correct one. That's why it's so effective to sell with emotion and justify with logic.

Calling to Action

According to Gerald Zaltman of Harvard Business School, 95% of purchase decisions are subconscious.[1] Our brains are massive super-computers, and our conscious mind is only a superficial layer. We will often rely on the processing power of the subconscious mind to feel our way to the right decision. The moment that we decide to buy, in our heart, is separate from the rational, logical justification that we make afterward.

In the Iowa Gambling Task Study, participants were given four decks of cards from which they were told to draw 100 cards total.[2] Some cards gave them rewards, and some gave them penalties. The participants played to win more rewards than penalties. What they didn't know was that the decks were stacked.

Some decks were preset to provide more rewards, while others were preset to give more penalties. After drawing about 80 cards, most participants figured out which was which. They could logically deduce which decks would give the maximum reward and drew their final 20 cards from the good decks.

After the first 10 cards, however, many people registered high levels of emotional anxiety when reaching for the bad decks. Their emotions warned them away from making bad decisions, even as their rational brain was still trying to figure things out. The gut instinct is guided by feelings, and not logic. That's why we need to separate the call to action from the buying decision.

- ✦ Call to action: Invitation to make a purchase

- ✦ Buying decision: Inner choice to make a purchase

1   Manda Mahoney, "The Subconscious Mind of the Consumer (And How To Reach It)," Research and Ideas, Harvard Business Review, January 13, 2003, https://hbswk.hbs.edu/item/the-subconscious-mind-of-the-consumer-and-how-to-reach-it

2   "Iowa Gambling Task," last modified December 21, 2021, https://www.psytoolkit.org/experiment-library/igt.html

The call to action appeals to the head. This gives you a logical, step-by-step method for exchanging value with someone else. But the buying decision is internal. It doesn't happen on a website or a contract or a checkout process. The buying decision is when your heart gives permission to your brain to proceed. The heart can even override your logic, if necessary.

If you can find a solution that satisfies both the Junkie and the Janitor, that's a sweet spot where you can make a compelling offer that people will buy. When you can't satisfy them both, the strategic move is to sell to the Junkie and not to the Janitor.

Logical Persuasion vs. Nonrational Influence

With an EEG monitor, we can measure what happens in our brains while we look at advertisements. Researchers published findings in the *Journal of Neuroscience, Psychology, and Economics* that measured neural activity of people viewing two different kinds of advertisements: logical persuasion and nonrational influence.[3]

Logical persuasion uses facts and figures to convince your head why a purchase makes logical sense. Nonrational influence uses evocative imagery associated with a product to get your heart to feel a certain way.

When viewing ads with logical persuasion, participants showed high activity in the regions of their brain that made decisions, such as the amygdala and the hippocampus. Evaluating benefits against risks and calculating numbers can prevent us from making bad impulse purchases.

Nonrational influence ads use lots of powerful imagery and little text. They don't provoke high neural activity in the decision-making parts of

3   Ian Cook, et.al., "Regional Brain Activation With Advertising Images." *Journal of Neuroscience, Psychology, and Economics*. 4. 147-160. 10.1037/a0024809. 2011.

our brains. This means buying resistance is lower when we're only being influenced emotionally.

If your brain is evaluating whether you should make a purchase, you're more likely to find reasons not to purchase. By providing logical facts and figures, we stimulate the part of the brain that encourages the inner Janitor to say no.

The emotional language of the heart decides whether we want to purchase, not whether we should. The decision-making parts of the brain are not as active. Our inner Junkie is ready to say yes, regardless of consequences.

The most startling truth is we don't even think our way to logical solutions. We feel our way to reason. Emotions are the substrate, the base layer of neural circuitry underpinning even rational deliberation. Emotions don't hinder decisions. They constitute the foundation on which they're made!

— Douglas Van Praet

Your head and your heart are each going to ask: Is this relevant? And, is this valuable? You get a positive buying decision by answering both of these questions for the head and the heart.

BUYING DECISION

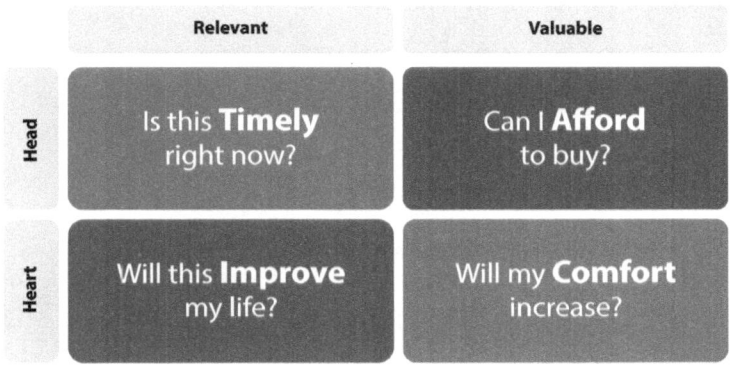

Logic doesn't convince us to buy; it only justifies the decision made by the heart.

Having logical reasoning on your sales page or in your brochure is nice, but if your call to action is only about money costs and time saved, your conversion rate on that page will be low. The best sales pages focus on status and happiness in the headlines and use logical justifications below the fold because we trust our emotions.

Logical reasons that don't evoke emotions don't easily trigger a purchase. You've heard the adages "sex sells," and "if it bleeds, it leads," right? When you create an emotional reaction, people are more likely to take action, even if the logical brain reasons against it.

To craft a message that persuades action, make pathos the priority. In Aristotle's Rhetoric, he defined the three elements of persuasion:

- ✦ Ethos — your character, experiences, and education
- ✦ Logos — your argument's logic and supporting evidence
- ✦ Pathos — the emotional connection you make with your audience

When business communication expert Carmine Gallo analyzed 150 hours of TED Talks, he found the most popular presentations contained 65% pathos, 25% logos, and 10% ethos.[4] Logic was not as persuasive or prevalent as emotional connection.

You can't just sell to the brain with a logical CTA. You also need to influence the Buying Decision, which is made through feelings.

The fastest way to the brain is through the heart.
— Gabrielle Dolan

---

4   Carmine Gallo, "Talk Like TED: The 9 Public-Speaking Secrets of the World's Top Minds," St. Martin's Press, 2014

Calling to Action

Look at your sales pages, promotional newsletters, and content marketing, and multiply the pathos. For every bit of logos in your positioning — for every statistic, justification, or logical reason that someone should buy what you're selling — try to complement it with two to three emotional rationales. Every bullet point for the inner Janitor should be surrounded by two to three points for the inner Junkie. If you can convince the heart first and the head later, you'll convince more people to make the buying decision.

ACTION STEPS FOR ELEVATING YOUR PLATFORM

Complete the exercises in the Cornerstone Workbooks at MarketingYourselfBook.com/workbooks:

SCAN ME

1. Duplicate one copy of the CTA Workbook for each offer. For different offers, use different copies.

2. Write answers to all the warm-up exercises.

3. Use these answers in the fill-in-the-blank formulas.

4. Copy winning phrases and sentences and paste them into the Copy Swipe section.

5. Practice sharing these CTAs with prospective customers, and update and edit them as you find what is most effective.

Cornerstone 3

Strategy

We are kept from our goal not by obstacles,
but by a clear path to a lesser goal.

— Robert Brault

A good strategy shows you what's working and what's a waste of time.

Without a good strategy, you could spend most of your effort going in the wrong direction, pursuing the wrong goal, and getting substandard results. Unless you have clearly defined goals and priorities, every shiny new marketing fad could distract you into a new and ineffective direction.

Your strategy becomes a litmus test for your decisions. Neil Gaiman gave a commencement speech where he talked about his goal to become a novelist. As a young writer, he imagined this goal as a mountain in the distance. Whenever he was presented with opportunities, like a job offer to become a journalist, he asked himself if this decision would take him closer to the mountain in the distance, or farther away. Journalism taught him to write concisely, which helps him as a novelist writing fiction decades later. He let his strategy guide him in making choices.

Strategy is not just deciding where to go, it's also readjusting to get there. When a boat that wants to travel 90 miles due east is blown off course by a storm, it doesn't continue going east no matter what. Circumstances may change around you. I promise, you will be surprised by the unexpected. Every entrepreneur has plans that fall apart, people who don't deliver on their promises, and a market that changes overnight. How well you handle these changes could mean the difference between success and defeat.

Your ability to readjust is guided by a fundamental understanding of your market, your capabilities, your customers, and their appetites.

Chapter 9

Research Competition for Shortcuts

Successful people leave behind clues. If you model what successful people do and stay persistent, then you should start seeing amazing results.

— Jeff Leighton

Being in business is like being lost in the woods. When you start your own business, you have to figure things out as you go. Nobody has ever run this new business before, so you have to find your way through the wilderness as best as you can.

Have you ever been lost in the forest? It's kind of exciting because the whole world is open for you to explore. You can go in any direction, and it almost doesn't matter which one you choose. If you strike out in a new direction, there's a chance you can discover a new vista that's never been seen by anyone else before. It does happen. I've been lost plenty of times, and I did have that happen once.

It was an amazing vista overlooking the city of Portland, Oregon. I was hiking with my good friend Eric, and we were lost in Forest Park for five hours. Forest Park is the largest park within city limits in the world, and we couldn't find our way out. For a while, we couldn't even find the rest of the city! After hours of searching, we discovered an amazing vista and saw the city from a completely unique angle. There are probably only a handful of people in the world who have seen Portland from that perspective.

Once we knew the direction of our destination, we knew which direction to push through the wilderness. But there were hills and valleys and undergrowth in the way. We were tramping through the underbrush, tired and dirty, for hours. Every step was a struggle. It wasn't until we found a trail that we were sure we would ever find our way out.

Follow the Path

I'll never forget the look on his face when Eric found the trail. One moment I was staring at my feet, dodging tangled roots, and suddenly I saw him up ahead, jumping up and down with a huge grin. With our feet on the path, we knew the way out of the wilderness. An hour later, we arrived where we wanted to go. All we had to do was follow in the footsteps of those who had gone before us.

Other entrepreneurs have found their way out of the same wilderness you're in right now. There are others who do what you do. Some of them even serve the same market as you. They're continually learning about your future customers. Their journey is full of insights, mistakes, and victories that create a path to the same destination where you want to arrive.

If you want, you can cut through the underbrush and forge your own path. It's dirty and grueling, and there is a limited chance of success. Or, you can make it easy on yourself and follow the trail left by others who have gone before you.

Walk It Yourself

Following someone else's trail is different than wearing their shoes while you do it. You can walk at your own pace, with your own rhythm, in the same direction. That doesn't mean you're plagiarizing those who walked before you. You won't be riding on their back. You'll be following the path of least resistance.

Sometimes when I share competition research techniques with people, they get concerned about authenticity. They worry that replication will make their business a copycat of their competition. But that's not what we're going to do. You will be doing your own work and using your own voice and brand, simply using inspiration from the voice and brand and actions of others further down the path than you are. Your journey will be easier if you follow in the footsteps of others, instead of fighting against the wilderness for every step.

The Three Types of Competitors

There are three types of competitors for any business:

- ✦ Direct competitors
- ✦ Secondary competitors
- ✦ Indirect competitors

Direct competitors serve the same market and solve the same problem the same way as you. Functionally, they're almost identical to you in the marketplace. The only differences to the customer are branding, price, and personality. McDonald's and Burger King are different, but not by much.

Secondary competitors have a different product or service, but they serve the same market as you do. The problem they solve is the same, but they go about solving it in a different way. Voodoo Doughnuts also sells food, but very differently than McDonald's. Secondary competitors teach you about the other ways your customers can solve their problems.

Indirect competitors serve the same market as you, but they satisfy a different need or solve a different problem. Their solution might be an entirely different product or service. Weight Watchers also solves hunger, but differently. Indirect competitors can alert you to changes in the market and are the most likely to become your best partnership opportunities.

THREE TYPES OF COMPETITORS

	Direct	Secondary	Indirect
Market	Same	Same	Same
Need	Same	Same	Different
Service	Same	Different	Different

Competition Case Study: McDonald's

Burger King sells the same product as McDonald's. They fill the same need for the same market: hungry people who want cheap, fast, tasty food. McDonald's and Burger King both sell burgers to hungry people who want to buy burgers.

Voodoo Doughnuts is different. They are a funky Portland-based doughnut shop that serves the same market (hungry people) and solves the same problem (I want something tasty to eat) as McDonald's. But they solve that problem with a different product. Sometimes, you don't want a burger. Sometimes, you want a bizarre doughnut that has bacon and maple syrup on it. (It's an amazing culinary master-piece that's disgusting and fantastic at the same time.) They are a secondary competitor to McDonald's. Same need, different product.

Weight Watchers is an indirect competitor to McDonald's. They serve the same market (people who need to eat). But there's a different set of needs for this market. They are not primarily concerned with eating something tasty. They make eating choices to lose weight. So, Weight

Watchers fills a different need with a different product mix, but they serve the same market of hungry people.

Weight Watchers might try a promotion or a launch that's really effective for hungry people, like offering a discount at a certain time of day, or rewarding you with extras for bringing a friend to eat with you. McDonald's can repurpose that strategy, if they're paying attention to their indirect competitors to keep a pulse on their market. The market for hungry people is big, and McDonald's can learn from the marketing and communications of all three types of competitors.

> *Competition makes you better, always, always makes you better,*
> *even if the competitor wins.*
> — Carlos Slim

Expanding Indirectly

Jonathan Klein, when he was the president of CNN, said he was more worried about the one billion users on Facebook than the two million users on Fox News. Think about that. His direct competitor, Fox News, provides the same service, filling the same need, to the same market. There's an indirect competitor over on Facebook, with a much larger user base. They have the same market (people who are consuming media), but they deliver a different product. Where do people go to get their news? Two million people are going to Fox News. But that's only a slice of the market share that goes to Facebook.

People are not using Facebook just to get news because it fills a different need. They go to Facebook to share photos, to keep in touch with their family, and to get the dopamine hits that social media provides. But if that is also the place where they end up getting their news, they won't be watching CNN. Also, there are many more Facebook users than there are Fox News viewers. If CNN wants to expand its reach, do you think that they'd be better off trying to poach some of the two million viewers from Fox News? Or would they be more effective by bringing some of those one billion users from Facebook over onto CNN?

We watch our competitors, learn from them,
see the things that they were doing for customers
and copy those things as much as we can.
— Jeff Bezos

Learn From Your Competition

Early in my career, someone gave me extremely helpful advice. He said to select three competitors at different levels of their business. Choose someone who is behind you, somebody at about the same level as you, and somebody ahead of you. Over the years, watch how their careers progress. Pay attention to their pivots. Observe how they develop over time.

I picked three people I wanted to be like and who shared similar qualities to me and my business. Over the years, I've watched them grow. Just by observing how they handle their transitions, what they try, and how they pivot, I've learned a lot. Not by copying them, but by observing the routes they choose and paying attention to their speed and progress.

If I see these people doing something clever after six months of their own customer research, I take note. If they stumble at a specific point, I watch out for hazards when I pass that way on my own journey.

By paying attention to others on my path, I can adapt their tactics for my own business (and learn from their mistakes) without spending months figuring it out on my own. I've learned more from my competition than I have from anything else I've ever done in my business.

Competition Research Case Study: Amber Vilhauer

There's a web designer I really like named Amber Vilhauer. We offer similar services to similar clients, providing digital marketing services for experts and entrepreneurs. I could have looked at her with envy and jealousy because, in many ways, she's a lot better than me. Instead, I reached out to her and said, "Hey, do you want to talk shop?" We ended up having a fantastic conversation.

She shared her pricing model with me, and it completely changed my business. I never would have learned this from talking to my audience. I could only have learned about this by talking to a competitor.

I told her how I typically charged my clients for website design projects: made an estimate for the project, took half the money down as a deposit, with the second half due on completion. I complained about having to sometimes chase down that final payment. And she said, "That's why I ask for payment in full, up front."

I was shocked. "Don't people give you resistance?" I asked her.

"Not once," she said. "I've been doing this long enough, I have great testimonials, and I have a high enough integrity with my work that I always deliver. Nobody has ever questioned my pricing model. And also, the clients that wouldn't agree to that arrangement are not the clients I want to work with anyway."

I was stunned. Then I realized: I have great testimonials, too. I have high integrity. I've been doing this for a long time. It made so much sense to me that I changed the pricing model for my digital marketing agency right away. From that moment on, I started taking payment in full, up front. And she was right; nobody complained.

My business became much more stable. I stopped having hectic revenue cycles dependent on when my clients paid their invoices. I started working only when my time was prepaid, and that was it.

This new change in my business worked out great. And I never would have upgraded my business in this way if I hadn't been willing to follow in the footsteps of my competition.

How to Research Your Competition for Fun & Profit

You can document the trail left by your competitors by keeping a swipe file. Swipe files are the secret to my success as a marketer. The reason I'm a good copywriter is because anytime I find copy (written content) that is exceptionally good, I save it in a swipe file.

Swipe files are shortcuts to get ahead. I don't copy and paste to plagiarize the work of others as my own because that's not what swipe files are for. I keep swipe files for creative assets I often produce, like email onboarding sequences, video scripts, brochures, and sales pages.

Whenever I'm ready to start creating a similar project, I start by looking at great examples for inspiration. This lets me harvest good ideas that are just lying on the trail, waiting for another entrepreneur to pick them up.

If you've never made a swipe file before, the Competition Research Workbook is an easy Google Doc you can use to save the best of the best content that you find out in the wild so you can review it whenever you're producing something similar. By researching your competition, you can create your own map out of the wilderness.

Most entrepreneurs are not aristocratic explorers packed with enough supplies for a long trip of unknown duration. They're often looking for another customer to fix their cash flow, and then another, and then another. Tramping through the wilderness might lead you closer to where you want to go, but you risk choosing the wrong direction and staying lost indefinitely. The surest method to find your way out of the wilderness is to follow a trail.

ACTION STEPS FOR ELEVATING YOUR PLATFORM

Complete the exercises in the Cornerstone Workbooks
at MarketingYourselfBook.com/workbooks:

SCAN ME

1. List your direct, secondary, and indirect competitors in the Competition Research Workbook.

2. Copy/paste their headlines and offers into your workbook.

3. Look up the book *Steal Like an Artist* by Austin Kleon if you feel uncomfortable.

4. Find new competitors using the tools in the workbook.

5. Make a list of lessons learned and future projects.

Chapter 10

Sell to Small Target Audiences

Reduce options. Increase focus. Multiply results.

— Carl Richards

Every time a coin landed in my guitar case, I smiled and sang, "Do you have a couch for me? I'm looking for a couch for free."

In 1997, I lived as a street musician for a year. I hitchhiked across North America and survived off of the kindness of strangers. Unlike many of my fellow hobos, I had a craft: I could play the guitar. Every day, I spent a few hours playing music in a public place. This earned me enough money for a day's supply of tacos and cigarettes. Sometimes, playing guitar also introduced me to people with couches.

If I'd held up a sign on the side of the road that said, "looking for couch," I would have slept outside more often than not. Instead, I offered value and made an impression first, before making my pitch. In sales terms, this enabled me to close more prospects in smaller numbers.

Busking Out to a Target Market

Because I had a musical instrument, I could attract people who liked to hear a stranger play music. These were often the same people who were most likely to let a stranger crash on their couch. I would let them know that I was passing through town and looking for a place to crash. Instead of sleeping outside every night, I often slept in spare bedrooms or on comfortable futons, because I was busking out to my target audience.

"Busking out" is a term from the world of street performance. When you pass a musician on a sidewalk who has a hat full of money on the ground, that person is busking out. They don't charge admission for their performance; they give the performance for free. As a reaction to that free performance, some people voluntarily pay for it.

Lunch and learns, free workshops, and infomercials are all examples of busking out. You provide interesting or useful content, and people pay with their attention. After collecting the attention of people who find your content interesting and useful, you make an offer.

Busking Out vs. Advertising

A random hitchhiker is a stranger, but a local musician is interesting. People who liked talking with new strangers were also those people most likely to pick me up as a hitchhiker. On a freeway on-ramp, I only had a few seconds to make an impression. My thumb, my posture, and the outline of my guitar case had to swiftly persuade my prospective chauffeurs. It was like the flash of an advertisement, and success was mostly a numbers game.

But busking out is different than advertising. Advertising works when a message reaches a large number of people, and it has a very low conversion ratio. Only a few people will follow the CTA in an ad, but with a large enough audience, the numbers can work out. With busking out, instead of grabbing attention from a large group in a flash, you earn a small group's attention for a little while. Once you have that attention, you get to decide what to do with it.

Case Study: Peter Cook Goes Busking Out

Peter Cook is a modern master of busking out for business. He has a three-hour workshop that he teaches to bookkeepers who want to grow their bookkeeping business. (Notice the clarity of that personal statement? Sticky, clear, and short.) Peter offers solutions to the specific and difficult challenges his market is facing for 2.5 hours, and then he spends 30 minutes pitching his 12-month program.

If Peter gave a 30-minute pitch to 12 bookkeepers individually, he could expect to close 10%–20% of those pitches. By collecting a group of prospects into one room, he spends less time selling by making a pitch to all of them at once. He front-loads the interaction with massive value to demonstrate his expertise — and closes 35% of his prospects.

Busking Out Is Smart Selling

Peter used this model when I met him, while he was busking out for Thought Leaders Business School. He came to Wellington from Melbourne and reached out to me beforehand on LinkedIn to offer to meet me for a coffee. When I said yes, he sent me a free copy of his excellent book, *The Thought Leaders Practice*. He also invited 80 other people to meet us for coffee, at the same time.

The presentation he gave was fantastic. It was well-targeted to the people in the room (coaches, speakers, authors, and trainers). At the end, he made an offer to join Thought Leaders Business School. I was one of the many people at his busk out who signed up for his program. Because he had already provided so much practical value, I knew the rest of his material was going to be great (and it was).

Four Simple Steps to Busking Out

If Peter had reached out to me on LinkedIn to sell me an expensive program, I would have ignored him. Instead, this is what Peter did:

+ Reached out and offered value

+ Sent an invitation to an interesting event

+ Provided massive value during that event

+ Closed with an invitation to purchase more value

Busking out is more efficient and effective than marketing broadly to a general audience. You can demonstrate expertise (and build trust) by solving simple problems for a narrow niche in a free presentation. After you impress these targeted prospects with your knowledge, they'll feel grateful for the value you've given them. This is the perfect time to make an offer to do business with you.

According to the *Harvard Business Review*, personalization reduces lead acquisition costs by as much as 50%.[1] This means if you can personalize your presentation to incorporate the specific details of people in the room, your revenue is likely to increase by 5%–15%. In the same study, they found that personalization increases marketing spend efficiency by 10%–30%.

Focus Your Best Marketing on Your Most Qualified Prospects

You can spend less money, smarter, by busking out to a targeted audience. While you could stand on a soapbox at the train station and try to convince a big crowd of strangers to listen to you, I can tell you from experience, this has a very low closing ratio. When I was busking out

---

1   Matt Ariker et al., "How Marketers Can Personalize at Scale," Marketing, Harvard Business Review, last modified November 23, 2015, https://hbr.org/2015/11/how-marketers-can-personalize-at-scale/.

with my guitar, sometimes a hundred people (or a thousand) would pass me by before I earned any coin.

Where I did really well was in small tourist towns. People were not commuting from one place to another. They were looking for something unique and interesting. I gave them what they were looking for, and then after volunteering value, I made a pitch.

This is the fundamental premise behind busking out. Give value first, then make an offer.

How can you provide massive value to a captive audience of qualified leads? These are the people who make the best customers. Qualified leads are people who actively demonstrate that they want what you're offering. Where can you find them in a group, and what would they find valuable? Figure this out, and your sales process will become much easier (and more entertaining).

ACTION STEPS FOR ELEVATING YOUR PLATFORM

Complete the exercises in the Cornerstone Workbooks at MarketingYourselfBook.com/workbooks:

1. Make a copy of the Busking Out Workbook to plan a free event or experience you could give away to your target market.

2. Schedule your busk out in your calendar.

3. Make a list of people to invite, and invite them.

4. Rehearse and perform and enjoy yourself.

5. Collect contact information with a survey or form.

6. Follow up with attendees one-on-one.

Chapter 11

Find the Buying Trigger

People hate to be sold, but they love to buy.

— Jeffrey Gitomer

The day was hot, and I was exhausted from running a five-kilometer obstacle course filled with mud pits and climbing nets. After 37 minutes on the Rugged Maniac course, I crossed the finish line, where a volunteer handed me a T-shirt, a medal, and a beer token. But what I really wanted was more water, and my bottle was empty. An enterprising young entrepreneur was nearby, sitting on a cooler full of ice-cold water bottles.

"Five dollars," he said with a grin, as he held one up and watched me drool. "Shut up and take my money!" I said.

Have you ever had this experience? You see something you want so badly, you're willing to pay top dollar for it immediately. The purchase will solve a problem so well, you're happy to throw down money right that very second. That's exactly what I did for that $5 bottle of water. I drank it in one long swig, and it was worth every penny.

Timing Is Everything

Ticket scalpers don't sell tickets at the grocery store. They sell them at the entrance to the stadium where the event is taking place. And with good reason. Their typical customer, their customer avatar, is someone who wants to get into the stadium but doesn't have a ticket. Waving tickets in the air at the stadium entrance is the best place for a scalper to sell a ticket to their customer avatar — and they can often do it for many multiples of the retail price.

If I'm shopping for avocados in the grocery store, I don't want to hear a pitch about why I should buy a ticket for an event over at the stadium. It's when I'm standing outside the stadium with a group of friends and they all have tickets and I don't that I'm facing a problem that needs a solution. A ticket scalper is exactly the person I want to talk to in that moment. That is a buying trigger.

Having a well-thought-out customer avatar helps you find the buying trigger. If you can find the people who are willing to say, "Shut up and take my money!" you can sell them what they want when they most want it.

Identify the Customer Avatar

A customer avatar is a broad, hypothetical representation of your future customer, and it has three main dimensions.

- ✦ The first is the demographic — who they are and what they're like.

- ✦ The second is the problem they face — the problem that you can solve.

- ✦ The third dimension is your competition - those who also study this demographic, and talk to them using phrases and topics that you can borrow.

And then there's your competition, which we talked about in chapter 9. Your competition has been studying this demographic and talks to them using phrases and topics that you can borrow.

CUSTOMER AVATAR

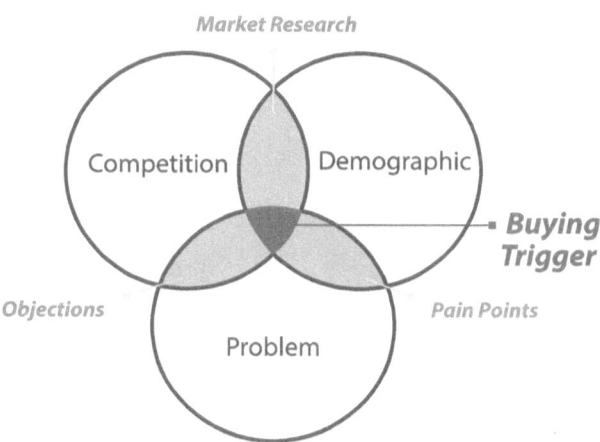

Your customer's pain points can be found in the overlap of the demographic and the problem. What problems do these people face regularly? If they were in a group together with their peers, what would they complain about? What resources do they share?

Market research helps you clarify your customer avatars.

Your competition has already been marketing to this demographic for some time, and they've figured out a few things. They know how your customers like to be spoken to, what they're likely to buy, and when. They've also learned how to anticipate and overcome the objections of your customers.

Follow their trail.

When Are You the Perfect Answer?

In the overlap of the objections, the pain points, and your market research, that's where you can find the clearest path to your offer, the buying trigger. I paid for an overpriced bottle of water because it was the perfect solution to a tangible problem I was facing right at that moment. My problem was so intense, the vendor didn't need to convince me of my thirst or the quality of his water or tell me his story. He just made an offer, and I happily accepted.

The buying trigger for a car mechanic is when your car starts making a funny noise or smokes or sparks or smells. If you're the customer avatar facing that problem, you're ready to do business right away. For a dentist, the buying trigger is a toothache. For an attorney, it's a broken contract. For a photographer, it's setting a wedding date on the calendar.

Determine when you can make an offer so that it's the perfect timing for your customer. How can you position yourself so you're ready at the moment of maximum discomfort? That is the moment when customers are most ready to buy from you. When you know the buying trigger, marketing yourself becomes easy.

According to a study by the *Journal of the Academy of Marketing Science*, impulse buying occurs 86% of the time when consumers are in a negative mood state, but only 38% of the time with a positive mood state.[1] Is there a negative experience your customer is facing at a time when your solution can become an impulse buy? Position yourself to provide a solution at the perfect time for your customer, like the vendor with a cooler of water bottles right next to the finish line.

Finding the buying trigger is a much more effective use of your time and energy than rewriting your About page or sending another newsletter. If you can realign your content around the problems your customers face and show them how to solve those problems, your marketing becomes much more effective. Becoming an expert in the problems of your customer helps you articulate the solution better than anyone else.

---

1   Gopalkrishnan Iyer et al., "Impulse buying: a meta-analytic review," *Journal of the Academy of Marketing Science*, 48, 384-404 (2019), https://doi. org/10.1007/s11747-019-00670-w https://www.researchgate.net/figure/ Results-of-moderator-analysis_tbl4_334351342

ACTION STEPS FOR ELEVATING YOUR PLATFORM

Complete the exercises in the Cornerstone Workbooks at MarketingYourselfBook.com/workbooks:

SCAN ME

1. Make a copy of the Customer Avatar Workbook.

2. Create three to four avatars with names and job titles.

3. Base one or two avatars on your best customers in the past.

4. Make one or two avatars based on customers you would like to have.

5. Identify the buying trigger for each.

6. Focus your marketing on the buying trigger.

Chapter 12

Make Your Marketing an Adventure

Make it simple. Make it memorable.
Make it inviting to look at. Make it fun to read.

— Leo Burnett

Your customer goes on a journey, like every hero in every story ever told. By using the framework of mythical storytelling, you can create a map for the journey your customer takes. This map guides strangers into becoming customers, leading them from the problem they face to the solution you provide.

In his classic book *The Hero with a Thousand Faces*, Joseph Campbell wrote about the monomyth, the story behind all stories. From *Beowulf* to *Star Wars*, he said, every great adventure follows the same Hero's Journey. The hero of the story goes through a specific series of meetings and challenges, and once you learn this progression, you can see it everywhere. This mythic structure has been used by countless authors as the framework for many of your own favorite stories. If your business applies the Hero's Journey to your customer journey, you can craft a compelling experience.

The secret is: make your customer the hero.

What Most Marketing Gets Wrong

Most marketing makes a bad mistake by assuming the role of the hero.

If you're marketing yourself, you're not Luke Skywalker. The customer journey is not your adventure. You are not the hero. The hero is your customer.

Your role is Obi-Wan. You are the wise mentor who equips the hero with the tools, the map, the mission, and the means to get to their goal. Your role is a supporting side character in the story of your customer. If you can stay out of the spotlight and make your customer the hero, they'll come to you when they need your help.

The Stages of the Hero's Journey

There are 12 stages of the Hero's Journey, as defined by Joseph Campbell, and later refined by Christopher Vogler, a screenwriter who adapted Campbell's work to screenwriting. *The Writer's Journey: Mythic Structure for Writers* has become a classic manual used by screenwriters to create a comprehensive adventure within a two-hour film. These 12 stages can be divided into a three-act sequence, with each act containing four story beats.

Act 1: Separation

When the hero begins their journey, they're in a world they know as normal. It might not be normal to the audience — it could be foreign or fantastic — but to the hero, their own world is ordinary. They escape the world of the common day for the duration of the story by eventually responding to a call to adventure. This separation, from the known to the unknown, is the first act of the Hero's Journey.

Story Beats for Act 1:

- ✦ Hero is in an ordinary world
- ✦ Hero gets a call to adventure
- ✦ Hero refuses the call
- ✦ Hero meets the mentor

Act 2: Descent

Upon leaving their ordinary world, the hero goes through a series of conflicts that raise the stakes. The problem could get bigger, or the chances of success could get smaller. Most of the story takes place in a special world, an unfamiliar environment, with unique challenges and difficulties.

Story Beats for Act 2:

+ Hero crosses the threshold to the special world

+ Hero encounters tests, allies, and enemies

+ Hero approaches the inmost cave

+ Hero overcomes a supreme ordeal

Act 3: Return

After the final battle, the story doesn't end. The hero has to return to the ordinary world, transformed. The hero who returns isn't the same hero who left in the beginning. The changes that have happened along the way solve the original problem.

Story Beats for Act 3:

+ Hero receives a reward

+ Hero embarks on the road back

+ Hero experiences a resurrection

+ Hero returns with the elixir

Now that you know the mythic framework of the Hero's Journey, let's overlay it upon the customer journey.

The Stages of the Customer Journey of the Hero

Act 1: Marketing

Remember, the first four steps along the Hero's Journey take place in an ordinary world. Before your future customer eventually embarks on an adventure (which is engaging with what you have to sell), they'll go through a predictable series of events that culminate with meeting you.

Story Beats for Act 1:

✦ Customer experiences pain points

✦ Customer becomes a qualified lead

✦ Customer has objections

✦ Customer is introduced to you

Act 2: Sales

The second act begins with crossing the threshold, when the customer exits their normal world full of problems. You're the one who shows them how to solve the relevant problem. There are obstacles within and without, inside and outside, and successfully navigating all of these obstacles to the purchase is the sales process.

Story Beats for Act 2:

✦ Customer has a discovery conversation

✦ Customer compares options

✦ Customer makes a buying decision

✦ Customer pays in a checkout process

Act 3: Service

The final third of this adventure begins with the reward. This is when the customer gains access to their purchase, whether that's because you emailed them your content or you shipped an item to their door.

The story isn't done when they buy from you, though. The story is done when they create other customers.

Story Beats for Act 3:

✦ Customer accesses purchase

✦ Customer uses purchase to solve the problem

✦ Customer experiences positive outcomes

✦ Customer tells others

Aberdeen wrote a brief calculating that 54% of the ROI for marketing was with the customer journey.[1] If you're not making a clear map of the journey from stranger to customer, you're leaving money on the table, plain and simple.

This map from stranger to customer can be useful, but maps are meaningless unless you can orient yourself to your current location. That's why every customer journey starts with the customer facing a problem.

1. The Ordinary World = Pain Points

Every hero starts in the world of the common day. Without an ordinary world to serve as the foil to the adventure, we don't know why the adventure is anything special.

When Frodo wanders around the Shire, enjoying its simple pleasures, we learn a reference point in his story in *The Lord of the Rings*. His extraordinary adventure ahead is contrasted with what he leaves behind in his ordinary world.

Similarly, your customer has a series of problems they're accustomed to facing that cause them difficulty. Many other people in the ordinary

1   Omer Minkara, "Customer Journey Mapping: Lead The Way To Advocacy," Aberdeen Group, November 2016

world just shrug and accept these problems and pains — but not your hero.

2. The Call to Adventure = Qualified Lead

When the hero decides they have had enough and is committed to making a change, that is when they accept the call to adventure.

When Katniss Everdeen watched her sister chosen by lottery for *The Hunger Games*, she could have stayed safely in the crowd. Instead, she volunteered as tribute, to take the place of her sister. This began the entire adventure, and without her accepting the call, there would be no story to tell.

While you could help just about anyone in the ordinary world, there is an action a prospect needs to take as a prerequisite before they become a qualified lead. This action might be requesting a quote or subscribing to your newsletter or experiencing a specific life event. If you can identify this critical step, you can encourage (or watch for) people in the ordinary world who are ready to answer the call to adventure.

3. Refusal of the Call = Objections

Refusing the call is how the hero ensures the adventure is worthy. It's common for heroes to immediately backtrack so they can review all the challenges ahead for the audience and clarify the stakes.

When Neo first talked to Morpheus in *The Matrix*, the agents had arrived in his office to take him away. Morpheus guided Neo to the scaffolding outside his building and gave him a choice: climb to the roof, or leave with the agents. Neo refused the call to adventure, came back inside, and was captured. The danger was too much to risk.

When your customer says, "I don't think this is really worth it," they're articulating reasons why they shouldn't do business with you. These objections are a natural part of the customer journey, and they don't mean the story is over. This friction ensures that the customer really wants to go on this adventure. They have to be willing to endure the risks if they want a chance of success.

4. Meeting the Mentor = Introduction to You

Arthur was an ordinary boy, living an ordinary childhood, until he met Merlin. The wise old mentor taught him the powers of Excalibur and revealed to him his destiny to withdraw *The Sword in the Stone*.

Your customer is living a smaller life, having a harder time than they could. They don't know how much better life could be — until they meet you. As the wise mentor, you can guide the customer through transformations that will improve their life for the better.

Describing these benefits, and challenging your customer to accept these changes, is what brings the customer out of Act 1: Marketing and into Act 2: Sales.

5. Crossing the Threshold = Discovery Conversation

Dorothy looked around the new world of Oz, where everything was unfamiliar. The tornado had taken her from the bland, ordinary world and brought her into a foreign land filled with bright colors and singing Munchkins. Her adventure to find the Wizard of Oz began in confusion.

The discovery conversation can take the form of an actual conversation or a whitepaper, sales brochure, e-commerce page, or pricing table. No matter the format, it's your opportunity to educate your customer about all the different solutions you have available. This material is the orientation that helps them make decisions about how they can do business with you. Expect them to be confused (and overwhelmed) at this stage of their journey, just as Dorothy was dazzled by the land of Oz.

6. Tests, Allies, & Enemies = Compare Options

When Harry Potter flies his broom onto the Quidditch pitch to earn points for Gryffindor House in *Harry Potter and The Goblet of Fire*, his enemies on the opposing team are supported by enemies in the stands. Throughout the game, he is tested by their schemes, and saved by his allies.

Your customer puts your offer through tests, comparing it to other options, researching your competitors, and talking with others in their life about this decision. Your offer is like the Golden Snitch, and it's hard for them to catch it if they are distracted. The greatest enemy always looms: doing nothing. Many customers leave the journey here. Paralyzed by choice, they could decide against continuing on if the decision is too confusing or difficult.

7. Approach the Inmost Cave = Buying Decision

Ethan Hunt describes a detailed heist to his elite team in every *Mission: Impossible* movie. Each obstacle is identified, described, and assigned a person to handle it. Everyone knows their part. They're ready to go.

This isn't where the climax of the story happens, but it is where the climax of the story is planned. This is where the buying decision happens, during this approach to the inmost cave. Before your customer finalizes their decision, they take time to review all the details and make sure they're doing the right thing.

8. Supreme Ordeal = Payment

When Aang fights the Fire Lord in *Avatar: The Last Airbender*, their battle scene alternates with a battle between the Fire Lord's children, Zuko and Azula. Just as the former pair are fighting for the fate of the world, the siblings are fighting for the fate of the Fire Nation. When it's time to tell of the supreme ordeal, even with multiple storylines, everyone goes through this phase of their journey at the same time.

For your customer, the supreme ordeal is the checkout process. It's the climax of the story, and it happens all at once. (Getting someone to pay three times is much harder, practically and emotionally, than bundling three transactions together into one purchase.) Are they able to pay you? Do they successfully complete the sales process? Does money change hands? Do they sign on the dotted line? This moment of decision is where the story becomes a success or failure.

If your customer survives the ordeal, they move into Act 3: Service.

9. Reward = Access Purchase

When Indiana Jones chooses the cup of a carpenter in *The Last Crusade*, he earns the Holy Grail. Once he grasps the reward he'd been seeking, he uses it to heal his father from a bullet wound, bringing him back to life. An earthquake separates him from his treasure, and he nearly plummets to his death trying to get it back. But he's told by his father, the fanatic who wanted the Grail more than anything, to let it go. Saving his son, he reveals that the true reward is their relationship.

After completing the purchase, there needs to be a stage of celebration when you reward your customer, too. This is their moment of triumph. The more memorable you can make this moment, the stronger the rest of their journey will be.

10. The Road Back = Solve the Problem

After serenading his parents to have their first kiss, Marty McFly leaves the school dance to go *Back to the Future*. His ordeal is complete — he has connected his parents and saved his own existence — but the adventure isn't over. He still has to travel 88 miles per hour and harness the lightning to get back home.

After they make their purchase, your customer will then return to where they started at the beginning of their journey, but this time, things will be different. Now that they have their reward, they'll be able to solve the problem they originally faced when the adventure started.

11. Resurrection = New Normal

When Joy returns to headquarters in *Inside Out*, Riley also returns home from running away. Both of these characters, inside and out, have returned to their ordinary world. This time, there's one critical difference, though: Sadness is no longer being suppressed. Sadness is given her rightful place as one of the five major emotions controlling Riley's life.

While your customer has gone on a journey to make this purchase from you, they still have one critical step remaining: implementation. If they do not install, use, or incorporate your purchase into their ordinary world, then they may as well have ignored the call to adventure. Ensuring your customers actually use your purchase is the gateway to the final stage, where you can gain the best kind of customers in the world: referrals.

12. Return = Tell Others

When Steve Rogers returns the Infinity Stones at the end of *Avengers: Endgame*, he doesn't return by traveling through time. He takes the long way back, living a quiet life (as a quiet Mr. Rogers, maybe). At the end of his long journey, he brings his legendary shield back, passing it to his friend Sam Wilson so he can become the next Captain America.

When your customer returns to their old life, they're changed by what they've bought from you. The problems that sent them on this quest are now solved, and adjusting to this new state will feel unfamiliar for a time. That's good because this period of unfamiliarity is the best time for them to share your works with other people like them.

The Customer Journey on Your Website

If you redesign your website to guide customers through the customer journey, you'll be rewarded as the guide of many quests. There is a page on your website that you could align with every stage of the customer journey. It looks like this:

1. Home

2. Subscribe

3. FAQ

4. About

5. Thank You

6. Case Studies

7. Product

8. Cart

9. Checkout

10. Members

11. Review

12. Share

If you don't have some of these pages on your website right now, make a note to create them. If the pages don't currently flow from one stage to the next, challenge your current pages.

✦ How could your Subscribe page lead to your FAQ page?

✦ How could your Thank You page lead to reviewing Case Studies?

✦ How could your Checkout page lead to a Members page?

✦ After someone gives you a review, are they given an automated option to share your expertise with others in their own ordinary world?

From *Star Wars* to *Moana*, from *The Matrix* to *Harry Potter*, all major modern blockbuster films have followed this journey. Providing your customer with a familiar map will help them follow you on an adventure to their purchase.

ACTION STEPS FOR ELEVATING YOUR PLATFORM

Complete the exercises in the Cornerstone Workbooks at MarketingYourselfBook.com/workbooks:

SCAN ME

1. Create a map for your future customers to follow with the Customer Journey Workbook.

2. Answer the questions in the workbook for each of the 12 stages of the customer journey.

3. Identify the active choices the customer makes to progress out of each stage of the journey and into the next.

4. Make a list of potential edits to your website that would encourage these steps.

5. Implement those changes on your website.

Cornerstone 4

Systems

*If you can't describe what you are doing as a process,
you don't know what you're doing.*

— W. Edwards Deming

Systems create exponential impact. Setting up a good system doesn't just impact the work in front of you. Your systems affect all of the working hours ahead of you, as well. Spending an hour doing your work has a finite return. Spending an hour setting up a system that saves you an hour every day will magnify your effectiveness.

It's hard for us to conceive the impact that systems can have on our lives, because our brains are just not built for it. "The greatest short-coming of the human race," according to physics professor Albert Allen Bartlett, "is our inability to understand the exponential function." Here's an example that just may break your brain.

Imagine that we played a game of chess together, and the winner was awarded an additional penny on every square of the chessboard. The chessboard has 64 squares in an 8 × 8 grid. On the first square, the winner gets one penny. On the second square, two pennies, and on the third square, three pennies. By the time we got to the 64th square, the winner would have a stack of 64 pennies. When you add up all the pennies in all the stacks on the chessboard, the winner would have 2,080 pennies, or just over 20 bucks.

Makes sense, doesn't it? That's a linear progression. Our brains can understand those numbers. But exponential numbers are more difficult to comprehend. Let's change the system, and I'll show you.

Instead of adding one penny to each square, let's say we doubled the size of the stack on the following square. The first square has one penny, the second square has two, but the third square has four. We double on the fourth square to get eight pennies, and by the time you finish the first row, the eighth square has a stack 128 pennies high. On the 12th square, you surpass 20 bucks, and by the 16th square, you have $327.68 in one stack. On the 32nd square, halfway across the chessboard, you would have $21,474,836.48, which would create a stack of pennies 1,334 miles high. By the time you got to the final square, your stack of pennies would reach 0.97 light-years off the planet. The value of all the pennies on the chessboard would be $184,467,440,737,095,516.15, more than 184 quadrillion dollars.

This example is adapted from the Wheat and Chessboard problem, which is nearly a thousand years old. Our minds can conceive of linear numbers, but after a simple change in the system, the numbers become incomprehensible. Instead of adding one penny every square, you double pennies for every square; that's just a change in the system.

Your work is linear and is limited by your time, but when you set up systems to automate work for you, your systems can help you grow exponentially.

Over the centuries, those who've learned this secret have applied the knowledge to creating systems beyond their personal capacity. That's what you are going to do, too, as you learn more about using systems to your advantage.

Chapter 13

Plan a Publishing Calendar

The key to content marketing is simple: all you have to do is show up and answer questions your right people are asking.

— Ash Ambirge

Publishing regularly creates ongoing brand awareness. Creating content helps people know you, then like you, and then trust you. Over time, your customers will develop the expectation to see you sharing the same things in the same way.

It may take some trial and error to discover the right cadence and the right content. Once you have a rhythm that you like, reliably publishing on a set schedule creates familiarity, comfort, and trust. If your audience can predict how you'll post, and you fulfill their expectations and continue to stay interesting, you'll achieve brand awareness.

When the Huffington Post first started, they published an average of one post on their blog every 58 seconds. James Clear, one of the most popular bloggers on the internet, posts once a week on his website. Your optimal posting frequency is probably somewhere in between.

B2B businesses spend an average of 28% of their marketing budget on content marketing. If you spend 1/4 to 1/3 of your marketing time creating and publishing new content, you're in the right range of effort and time spent.

How often should you publish new content? The frequency you post is a matter of both stamina and style. Your publishing capacity is balanced against the appetite of your audience. Finding the right balance can be tricky. Post too much, and you'll get unfollows and unsubscribes. Post too little, and people will forget who you are.

You can post — short form to social media, long form to your website — every month or every week or every day. You could manually upload unique content to every network or syndicate one template post across multiple channels. The choice is always up to you.

But to clarify your activity, ask yourself: Do you know your content marketing goals?

Publishing Content Has a Purpose

If you don't know the purpose of your content, it's going to be difficult to find the right cadence for your publishing. Typical goals for content marketing include publishing content to:

1. Build brand awareness

2. Generate new leads

3. Nurture your relationship with your audience

4. Sell your products or services

These four goals follow the 4-Step Marketing Cycle of Know, Like, Trust, and Buy. You may want to focus on one of these four goals more than the others, depending on your current goals. So, to answer the question, "How often should I publish?" first pick one of the four goals above.

After you've picked one of those four goals, answer these questions: How often do you like to publish? Are you a daily poster? A weekly writer? A monthly publisher? Do you feel like you show up too much or too little? Your personal preferences are an important factor. If you can weigh your own preferences against those of your audience, you'll find a point of balance.

Daily deals websites like Groupon can email their audience every single day because they offer immediate, time-sensitive information. But a local auto mechanic, for example, would be hard-pressed to produce daily content. HubSpot discovered that Facebook pages with less than 10,000 fans had a 50% drop in engagement per post when posting more than once per day.[1]

Here's a good rule of thumb: publish a post on social media once a day and publish your newsletter once a week. If you like to write more than that (or less than that), find the cadence that works best for you. Your audience will tell you through their engagement, or the lack of it, whether it's working.

One of the greatest aspects of being an entrepreneur is that you get to decide how often you'll show up to your audience. You can suddenly show up when the mood and the moment strike you. Or you can carefully consider what you'll say and when you'll say it.

PUBLISHING STYLE

Impact

x12	Predictable	**Consider** What + When
x8	Prepared	**Consider** What to say
x4	Planned	**Consider** When to publish
x2	Reflective	**Suddenly** Sharing personal details
x1	Responsive	**Suddenly** Replying to comments
-1	Reactive	**Suddenly** Random

1 Lindsay Kolowich Cox, "How Often Should You Post on Facebook?" Last updated September 10, 2020, https://blog.hubspot.com/marketing/facebook-post-frequency-benchmarks

When you consider in advance what you'll say and when you'll say it, your publishing style can be planned, prepared, and predictable.

If you suddenly publish because something compels you to respond, or you react in the moment, you won't be nearly as effective. Your audience won't know what to expect from you. Anytime you do post, it will be a surprise.

Having a weekly newsletter is an example of a reliable pulse your audience can count on. A short, weekly message is enough to stay top-of-mind. If you encourage your audience to reply or take an action, you may get lucky and discover that this is the specific week they're facing the exact problem that you happen to solve.

Here's a secret about email newsletters: open rates do not accurately predict results. Just by sending a newsletter, you're inserting your name into someone's inbox; they don't have to open it. Reading your subject line and seeing your name is enough for them to briefly recall who you are and what you do. This might be enough to jog their memory when they need to solve a problem in your area of expertise or refer you to a friend, even if they delete your email without reading it.

Separate Writing Time From Posting Time

When I'm in writing mode, I spend a lot of time generating new content. That mindset is very different than the mechanical mindset that sends the newsletter or uploads the video. Publishing requires lots of small decisions. You have to decide where to post, what time to post, what tags would make your post searchable, whether the post needs an image, how to get that image to display properly, how to get the right tracking parameters on the link ...

There are so many mechanics involved in how you post. It will be more efficient to separate that activity from deciding what you post.

Set aside some time to write a lot of ideas that your customer avatar would find valuable. Collect a bunch of snippets, passages, and thoughts into a single, messy document. Then, using an automated posting tool like Buffer or HootSuite or Hypefury, edit and schedule these posts to go out in the future. Do this mechanical posting separate from composition.

Two great things about auto-posting tools are:

- ✦ They let you modify the frequency of how often you post.

- ✦ They analyze the effectiveness of your previous activity.

- ✦ I suggest you do an experiment: spend a week posting three times a day on Twitter, and then another week posting once per day, and then compare the results to discover what works best for your audience.

Publishing Regularly Has Long-Term Benefits

I've had people book marketing consultations with me (seemingly out of the blue) because they started following me on Twitter six years ago. I post frequently on social media, and it's a business strategy. When people need to hire or refer someone like me, I might be the first one they think of because they saw me post a funny picture of my dog that day.

According to a study by Forrester, an average of 11.4 pieces of content need to be consumed before someone makes a purchase.[2] Wouldn't it be easy to automate a lot of those points of contact through Buffer? You don't need to send a dozen thoughtful, well-written posts to every single person individually. Automation tools allow us to compose all of our content in advance and have it dripped out over time.

---

2   Ryan Skinner, "Brief: Marketing And Media Efficiency Outcomes Drive Content Marketing," Forrester, last modified September 14, 2015, https://www.forrester.com/report/Brief-Marketing-And-Media-Efficiency-Outcomes-Drive-Content-Marketing/RES128042

Talk to your audience as a general group. Compose the type of message that many of them would find useful, relevant, or interesting. According to Sprout Social, most brands post on social media an average of 0.97 times per day, and they have an engagement level of .09%.[3] That's a lot of activity, with only a faint level of connection. These numbers work better as your audience grows.

In 2018, Social Media Examiner conducted a survey of professional marketers, who said they saved an average of six hours per week by using automation tools.[4]

Marketing yourself should be a key component of your regular workflow. But you don't want to fall down one rabbit hole after another, chasing the next shiny thing. Creating and sharing your content shouldn't take all of your time, but saving too much time on social media can burn your relationships. The promise of technology is that you can reach anyone, anywhere, anytime. But does this communication strengthen a relationship, or damage it?

Mechanical Responses

Chatbots sound like they're new and cutting edge, but the first chatbot was built way back in 1966 by Joseph Weizenbaum at MIT. This bot was named ELIZA, and it was one of the first artificial-intelligence programs capable of taking the Turing test. The Turing test is a series of questions you can ask a computer to demonstrate whether or not it can think like a human.

ELIZA could take the Turing test, but couldn't pass it. This bot was only able to simulate conversation. After you said things to the computer program, the chat-based text interface would give you a variety of

3   Brent Barnhart, "41 of the most important social media marketing statistics for 2022," Social Media Trends, Sprout Social, last modified March 22, 2022, https://sproutsocial.com/insights/social-media-statistics/.

4   Michael Stelzner, "2018 Social Media Marketing Industry Report," Social Media Examiner, last modified May 7, 2018, https://www.socialmediaexaminer.com/social-media-marketing-industry-report-2018/

different answers. But ELIZA wasn't capable of learning from interaction. What you said to the program didn't alter its future behavior, and that limited its ability to mimic actual human conversation.

After five decades, chatbots have come a long way. In companies of 1–50 people, using chatbots has been shown to cut customer service costs by 30%.[5] Sounds great, right? Having a computer handle all those mundane service requests can save time and resources, but automating a relationship can also have unintended consequences.

A study of 6,200 customers of financial services firms found that using chatbots lowered sales by 80%.[6] It's true that using chatbots saved time, because humans on staff would not have to handle incoming service requests. However, they also lost the opportunity to ask follow-up questions. The firm's ability to cross-sell other services was drastically reduced.

	Authenticity	Automation
Time	80%	20%
Medium	Phone	Email
Impact	High	Low
Answers	Q&A	FAQ
Investment	Time	System

5 "AI chatbot that's easy to use," Products, IBM, accessed April 28, 2002, https://www.ibm.com/products/watson-assistant/artificial-intelligence
6 Gil Press, "AI Stats News: Chatbots Lead To 80% Sales Decline, Satisfied Customers And Fewer Employees," Enterprise & Cloud, Forbes, last modified September 25, 2019, https://www.forbes.com/sites/gilpress/2019/09/25/ai-stats-news-chatbots-lead-to-80-sales-decline-satisfied-customers-and-fewer-employees/

Authenticity vs. Automation

Relationships require an investment of time. People can tell when you try to cut corners on building a relationship, and it cuts off the relationship. Automation only gives the illusion of customer service. It's true, you can automate the simplest steps in growing and maintaining a relationship. But if you don't balance that automation with authentic connection, people will treat you like a bot.

The biggest problem with automation is it can create negative experiences that you never hear about. When someone gets frustrated with your chatbot, or sneers at your automated email message, does it make a sound? Studies have shown that 12 or more positive experiences are needed to make up for one unresolved experience.[7] Automation is necessary to stay productive, but too much can damage your relationship with your audience and your customers.

Consider the difference between answering a robocall and a personal call. Imagine answering your phone, and you're greeted by an automated voice message. There's very little incentive for you to give your full attention or to follow its instructions. But if someone calls you personally and asks for you by name and takes time and effort to engage with you as a human, it's much more likely that you'll listen to what they have to say.

You may have been sent an automated birthday card before. SendOutCards is one of the internet companies that automates the printing and sending of birthday cards. And I don't know about you, but I've always found those a little disingenuous. I'm a lifelong sender of handwritten notes. I believe that the time and effort it takes to handwrite a note has a much greater impact than something I clicked to send in a moment.

7 Glance, "Counting the Customer: The Complete Guide to Dynamite Customer Care," http://ww2.glance.net/wp-content/uploads/2015/07/Counting-the-customer_-Glance_eBook-4.pdf

Plan a Publishing Calendar

These are the two clear differences between authenticity and automation: time and effort. If you can balance authenticity against automation, you can communicate with a lot of people quickly.

Spending time and effort on a relationship counts in your favor when courting someone new, but if it's apparent you've invested neither effort nor time, they'll feel free to ignore you in return.

Too Much Automation Ruins Your Authenticity

When I see someone has put in time and effort — through referencing something I recently published or making a joke about something funny in my LinkedIn profile — I'm willing to give a cold request a bit of extra attention as a reward. But if I can tell, at first glance, that a request is fully and totally automated, I know I can safely ignore it.

Here's an example: I subscribe to newsletters with my first name in all caps (CAELAN). Since I'm a marketer and I study email marketing, I subscribe to a lot of newsletters. One day I received a message in my inbox that said, "Hi CAELAN, it's real Mindy, not robot Mindy :o)"

Three days after I subscribed to her list, I got an automated email masquerading as an authentic email. I could immediately tell, because of how I subscribed to her system — in all caps. My new relationship with her was revealed to be completely inauthentic.

On the other hand, I once subscribed to a fellow marketer's email list, and they asked me to reply to their welcome email and tell them my biggest challenge. We started a back-and-forth dialogue that became an authentic relationship.

I'm using email as the example here because I like email. (I have so many unread messages because I like to learn from other email marketers and stay on top of what they do.) You might prefer DMs on Instagram or SMS or Telegram. I personally can't stand those channels, but everyone has different preferences, and you should use what makes you feel comfortable.

Where You Do Well Is a Matter of Your Style

The variety of communication platforms can be overwhelming. So I recommend that you pick one platform where you show up authentically and automate the rest. Follow the 80/20 rule: spend 20% of your time automating 80% of your posts, and spend 80% of your time on the authentic 20%.

Automate what you can, but stay authentic where it matters.

You can specialize in your favorite social media platform. Automatically republish onto all the other accounts on future days. All you need is a system.

I post across multiple accounts every week with 30 minutes of dedicated focus. By using a Repurpose Matrix (which you can find in the Content Calendar Workbook), I can spend half an hour crafting 30–60 posts across six different social media platforms. Those 30 minutes are when I create the Ghost in the Machine.

You can't broadcast a TV show on every channel at the same time. Syndication will change how often reruns are shown to an audience. If you have one show on one channel at one time, you can have it delivered to other channels at different times.

That's what a Repurpose Matrix does. It plans out your content in advance. You can decide when and where your posts will be syndicated elsewhere. Creating a Ghost in the Machine does take some time and effort, but once your automation system is ready, you can preserve your attention and creativity for what's most important: creating authentic content.

ACTION STEPS FOR ELEVATING YOUR PLATFORM

Complete the exercises in the Cornerstone Workbooks at MarketingYourselfBook.com/workbooks:

SCAN ME

1. Plan a year of content with the Content Calendar Workbook.

2. Copy/paste listed items into content formulas.

3. Edit content for voice and flow.

4. Plan daily, weekly, and monthly content publishing schedules.

5. Distribute content into planned posts using an auto-posting tool or an assistant.

Chapter 14

Show Off Your Showroom

If you can figure out how to get people to consume your content for free, you are 80% of the way there to being able to sell it. Attention is far more scarce than money.

— Tiago Forte

The moment I stepped into the store, I felt something was wrong. My wife and I were strolling down Hawthorne Street in Portland. Our young kids were at home with their grandmother, and we were on our first date in a long time. Walking along the lively street, we entered a store that looked interesting from the outside. There was lots of art hanging in the windows, displays of candles and books, and little statues of fairies and wolves. (We're Portlanders at heart; we like that kind of store.)

As we stepped inside to browse, the shopkeeper was staring at us. "Hello," I said.

"Can I help you find anything?" she demanded with a frown.

I shrugged. "No, we're just looking." We wandered through the store, chatting about things we found interesting.

After a few minutes, we returned to the door, still chatting, enjoying our date. When we opened it, the shopkeeper demanded once again, "Can I help you find anything?" As I held the door open for my wife, I looked at the shopkeeper over my shoulder, confused by her question.

"No," I said. "Thanks. Have a nice day." She scowled at me as we left.

Out on the sidewalk, my wife and I talked about the strange experience. We like the kinds of things she had for sale in her store. There were plenty of things we could have purchased. But the shopkeeper didn't make us feel welcome.

I've had similar experiences online. After subscribing to someone's newsletter, the very first email demands to know how they can help. But I don't know yet. Right after subscribing, I often don't know what I need, or even what I'm looking for. I'm just browsing.

Take a Look Around

When someone subscribes to your newsletter, it's like they're wandering into your shop for the first time. For a digital business, your email confirmation saying "Welcome to my list!" is the welcome mat into your showroom. People agree to enter your corner of the internet and voluntarily signal that they're willing to browse your offers. This is your best opportunity to show future customers around your little shop.

Imagine if that shopkeeper had welcomed us with a smile and said, "We just got some new books in, over on that wall. What kinds of books do you like?" I would have happily told her all about my interests, and she could have learned about the sorts of things that she could sell to me easily.

Your new subscribers can be treated the same way. Right after they confirm their subscription, fresh email subscribers are the most open to learning about your brand, your offers, and your story. Make your new email subscribers feel welcome. (I'm going to use email as my example here, because it's been popular and effective for the last decade. If things are different when you're reading this, adapt these concepts to your current tools.)

"The very first email you send to a new subscriber sets the tone for how they see you for the rest of their time with you," says Naomi

Dunford, founder of IttyBiz.com, "so you want to get this one right. It's also the single best email for getting them to look at specific pages of your site, like popular posts or product pages."[1]

Most businesses just set up a default confirmation email that says, "Thanks for subscribing to my list!" and leave it at that. Imagine this happening in someone's shop. The little bell rings. You walk in and wipe your feet on the mat. The shopkeeper says, "Thanks for coming in!" and disappears into the back. It's up to you to browse through the shelves, develop questions, and decide to make a purchase. All on your own.

Now, imagine the best kind of experience you've had in a store. The shopkeeper asks good questions, makes recommendations, guiding you seamlessly to what you should do next. Before you know it, you're at the counter pulling out your wallet as your purchases are being bagged. That's what an email welcome series can do for customers.

Know, Like, and Trust via Who, What, and How

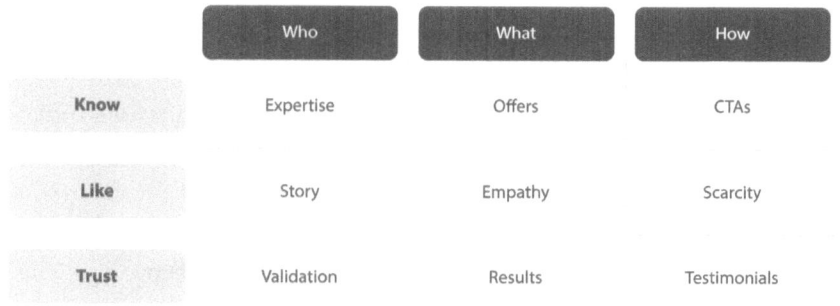

	Who	What	How
Know	Expertise	Offers	CTAs
Like	Story	Empathy	Scarcity
Trust	Validation	Results	Testimonials

New email subscribers get to know who you are when you share your expertise. They like who you are when you share your stories, and they trust who you are when you validate your promises to them.

1   Naomi Dunford, "The Ultimate Digital Marketing Template Pack," February 21, 2020, https://ittybiz.com/marketing-template-pack/

After they've read a few of your emails, they learn what your offers are. If you tell good stories, they'll develop empathy for the characters in those stories. If you can demonstrate results, they'll trust your methods.

Clearly describing how to do business with you is accomplished by a CTA. CTAs can be difficult to write in the moment, so it's helpful to compose them in advance. (My Promo Copy Workbook can help you there.)

You can inflate the value of your offers by introducing scarcity. If this is the only time to buy something at this price, or if your calendar will be filled after the available spots are taken, people will be more interested.

Finally, third-party validation of your effectiveness is the best way to build trust. Provide testimonials in your email onboarding sequence, and you can set up a system that automatically converts the right strangers into customers.

Remember that number from Forrester Research: an average of 11.4 pieces of content need to be consumed before someone will make a purchase from you. Your email onboarding sequence can make many of those touches for you automatically.

Case Study: Welcome Email Series From ClairePells.com

Content strategist Claire Pelletreau has an evergreen program she promotes in her email onboarding sequence. But she doesn't pitch it right away.

She starts with mentioning a tripwire (which we'll cover in chapter 15) and provides a lot of value through her Know-Like-Trust emails. Her sequence is a great example of a slow burn, building a relationship before making an offer:

1. PDF delivery + pitch for tripwire, includes countdown timer in email

2. Know-Like-Trust email

3. Know-Like-Trust email

4. Know-Like-Trust email

5. Second pitch for tripwire, includes countdown timer in email

6. Know-Like-Trust email

7. Know-Like-Trust email

8. Know-Like-Trust email

9. First email pitching the bundle, includes countdown timer

10. Second email pitching the bundle, includes countdown timer

These frequent Know-Like-Trust emails provide value, answer unasked questions, and deepen the relationship. "When I finally upgraded to a paid plan with Mailchimp," Claire said, "and sent new subscribers a series of emails that shared my top blog posts, my story, and links to my services and course pages, I started getting a lot more clients and customers."[2]

Notice how she alternates value with selling. She provides value more frequently than she sells, which gives her the credibility to make offers.

If a shopkeeper educates you with some free advice, it lowers your resistance to messages that sell. According to a study by Conductor,

---

2 Claire Pelletreau, "How to Build an Evergreen Sales Funnel with ConvertKit," last updated December 18, 2019, https://clairepells.com/evergreen-sales-funnel-convertkit/

consumers are 131% more likely to make a purchase after consuming educational content.[3]

Here are some best practices you can follow with your email welcome series:

1. Set expectations with your automated welcome email

After someone subscribes to your list, you can tell them you're going to email them again in three days with a message about whatever the topic is. When your email onboarding system automatically sends that message, the fulfillment of that expectation builds trust. Be clear about the kind of content they can expect to receive and what you'll be asking them to do.

2. End every automated welcome email with a single CTA

Every email in your onboarding series should have a call to action at the end. It's best to have just one because if you provide too many choices, your user will take none of them. If an email in your onboarding series has multiple calls to action (Read this article! And that one! And buy this thing, too!), you can split that up into different messages and send them on different days.

3. Invite connections across platforms

Email is only one of the many channels we use to communicate online. In recent years, it's been the most effective, but if you're also active on Twitter or YouTube or Medium or somewhere else, invite your new subscribers to follow those accounts, too. Talk about what you like about your favorite platforms, why you prefer this one over others, and link to one of your best-ever posts. This provides an extra autoresponder email that helps people Know, Like, and Trust you.

---

3 Charity Stebbins, "Educational Content Makes Consumers 131% More Likely to Buy," Spotlight, Conductor, last modified July 6, 2017, https://www.conductor.com/blog/2017/07/winning-customers-educational-content/

4. Tell stories of other satisfied customers

Show empathy with the problems your subscribers face and describe the results your clients have achieved. Telling stories and highlighting case studies will help your new subscribers to self-identify as someone who could be one of your customers, too.

5. Provide value at least as often as you sell

If you don't alternate value with sales, your unsubscribe rate will be high. Not many brands can get away with sending sales messages every day. If you're gaining new subscribers with lead magnets (which we'll go over later in this section), then your list is made up of people who want to learn how to solve a specific type of problem. Continue providing solutions to them at least as often as you send sales messages.

6. Offer clear instructions on how to do business with you

An email onboarding sequence helps subscribers know what you offer by automatically sending information about your best-selling (or highest-profile) offers. They'll only know about these offers if you're willing to share specific and clear instructions on the next steps. (If you need help clarifying these next steps, make a customer journey map using the framework in chapter 11.)

> *There's no such thing as 'hard sell' and 'soft sell.'*
> *There's only 'smart sell' and 'stupid sell.'*
> — Leo Burnett

While I've used email as the mechanism for communication in this chapter, you can still automate positive touchpoints with your customer using other methods. At specific milestones along the customer journey, no matter what technology you use, you can share stories and invitations automatically.

Is Your Welcome Mat Dusty?

How long has it been since you subscribed to your own email newsletter or tested your purchase process with a dummy account?

One of the first things I do when I start working with a new client is an Onboarding Audit. I use a testing email address to subscribe to their email newsletter or buy their product or join their community. After a couple of weeks (if their welcome series even goes that long), I run a search on my inbox for that testing email address, and I can see the entire welcome series just as a new subscriber would see it.

You can create your own testing email address if you know how to create email forwarders. Set up an email address like testing@your-domain.com. Or, if you have a Gmail address, you can simply add "+testing" to your handle (like myaddress+testing@gmail.com, where "myaddress" is your current Gmail handle), and it will still go to your Gmail inbox.

If you already have a newsletter list, what I'd like you to do, right now, is subscribe to your own email newsletter with a testing email.

Next week (or tomorrow, if your autoresponder sequence is just one email), take a look at what your new subscribers see. Ask yourself: How can I be the best shopkeeper? How can I show them around? What can I send them at the start of our relationship?

Use my Stellar Email Template if you need some fillable formulas to flesh out your email copy. My simple welcome email template for new subscribers has copy-paste formulas for follow-up emails that promote your offers and your best posts.

ACTION STEPS FOR ELEVATING YOUR PLATFORM

Complete the exercises in the Cornerstone Workbooks at MarketingYourselfBook.com/workbooks:

SCAN ME

1. Make a copy of the Stellar Email Template.

2. Replace all content in CAPS, edit the content and sending times to match your style and your voice.

3. Transfer the content to your email service provider.

4. Schedule the email automation.

5. Subscribe to your own list to see how it looks in your own inbox.

6. Review and edit every three months.

Chapter 15

Steps on a Value Ladder

Build an audience, and sell 'em what they want.

— Derek Halpern

The steps on a Value Ladder help you sell in sequence. The biggest sales are rarely the first purchase of a brand-new customer. Have you ever been offered a free sample in a grocery store? Maybe it was a bite of a bagel or guacamole or a little sausage on a toothpick. Something small. Something new and interesting. Something free.

After taking a bite, were you asked to become a shareholder in that company? Were you asked to become a distributor and turn your garage into a warehouse full of their product? Were you asked to take out your phone and tell your friends and family about it? Probably not. At most, you were offered the chance to put something new into your shopping cart. This is the power of free samples — they can quickly gain you little sales, but they rarely get you big sales right away. That's why you may find it helpful to build a Value Ladder.

From the Bottom to the Top

Would you pay $10,000 for an hour of someone's time? If you met someone, shook hands, and traded business cards, if they offered you a $10,000 coaching session right away, I'm fairly certain the answer would be no.

But still, some coaches can charge $10,000 an hour for their time. They can do this by making ascending offers in a Value Ladder. By slowly increasing trust (and price) with a series of ascending offers, they earn the right to make bigger pitches. Ideally, you're only offering your top-shelf, premium services to your raving fans.

A Value Ladder helps you sell without feeling sleazy. Offers start small at the bottom, with an easy ask. "Subscribe to my newsletter to get this free PDF" is a typical offer. I'm sure you've stepped onto someone's Value Ladder this way before. It may even be how you started following me — by subscribing to get one of my lead magnets, like the Personal Branding Checklist or the Marketing Automation Checklist or the Zoom Host Checklist.

These are the first steps on my Value Ladder, and they're valuable evergreen assets. I can offer these PDFs in communities of people who would find my services valuable, and the right people will subscribe to my newsletter to get them. The next step on a Value Ladder is the tripwire — an easy, non-threatening microcommitment.

From Subscribers to Buyers

A tripwire is a low-priced offer that segments your audience into subscribers and buyers. Buyers are a different segment of your audience. These are people who have demonstrated a willingness to pull out their credit card (or cryptocurrency wallet) and pay you.

In an email onboarding series, it's common to offer a tripwire with a discount to your new subscribers. A recent popular promotion is to offer a $47 product discounted to $7 if purchased directly after an email subscription.

The tripwire can help you identify the buyers on your list, and you can talk to them differently than your main list as a whole. This exclusive group of proven buyers within your audience will be open to hearing your calls to action more frequently, and they'll convert into customers more often than strangers because you already have a commercial relationship.

Case Study: The Value Ladder of Tony Robbins

Business strategist Tony Robbins has a podcast. It's free, it's public, and anyone, anywhere, can listen to it. This podcast lets strangers get to know him and his work. In addition, he also has a free online course called Business Mastery. To get access to this free course, you have to subscribe to his newsletter. Immediately after signing up for this course, you're offered a tripwire for $12.95: the RPM Monthly Calendar.

Every step of the Value Ladder, you're exposed to higher offers:

+ $299 — Personal Power 30-Day Course

+ $995 — Unleash the Power Within Live Event

+ $10,000 — Mastery University Conference

At the end of his mid-priced live event, you'll be treated to a masterful sales pitch for his high-priced offer. But you won't hear that sales pitch after buying the tripwire. You won't hear that pitch after subscribing to the free course. He's not trying to close his podcast listeners for a $10k sale because they're still too far down the Value Ladder.

Each step in the Value Ladder upsells what's one step above, because it's easier to ask people to open their wallet a little more than to ask them to open it all the way.

VALUE LADDER

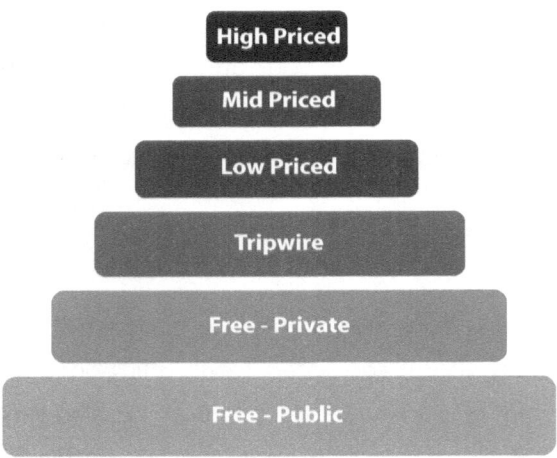

How To Organize Your Offers Into a Value Ladder

✦ Make a list of everything you can sell, both now and in the future.

✦ Categorize these offers into six categories:

    ✦ Free – Public

    ✦ Free – Private

    ✦ Tripwire

    ✦ Low-Priced

    ✦ Mid-Priced

    ✦ High-Priced

✦ Starting from the top of your Value Ladder, work backward. How can you make an offer to one step up from the step just below?

- ✦ Define the transitions between all the stages. Go into your systems and encourage people to take the next specific step up the Value Ladder.

- ✦ Update your email autoresponders, your website copy, your selling scripts, and your notifications to upsell.

- ✦ Create a dummy testing customer and go through the entire sequence yourself. Take notes during the testing, but don't make edits until you get to the end.

Once you see your entire Value Ladder in one list, you might get ideas for cross-selling from one offer to another. You might notice that some offers are good for one audience or customer avatar, while another set of offers is completely different. Some platforms require different Value Ladders, and that's fine. Everything can seem messy from your perspective, but if your offers are streamlined in a natural progression for your customer, it works great.

Solve a Small Problem With a Lead Magnet

I'm sure that once upon a time, you faced a problem. It was a minor inconvenience. You didn't want to pay somebody to fix it, and you were willing to do a little bit of research to figure out how to fix it yourself. After going to Google for a few answers, you discovered that this problem was actually much more complicated than you thought. Since it may be a big project, you settled in for a few minutes of research.

You had plenty of information available; each of the websites you opened was full of material. Some were detailed tutorials with lots of advertisements crowding out the free information. Some were simple landing pages, with a promise and a form, asking for your email address.

While you are in the DIY research phase, you might watch a YouTube tutorial, or click an ad for a free course. Maybe you subscribe to an email list to get a free PDF. This might solve your problem completely, or it could reveal how much more work there is to be done.

The larger and more complicated the problem, the more time you're required to invest in solving it. This makes it more likely that you'll change that investment from time to money.

Earn Trust Before Asking for Money

In the internet age, nobody faces the problem of "not enough information" anymore. All of the world's information is available to anyone with an internet connection. But there's a different problem that we all share. It's some variation of, "How do I find the specific information I need to solve this problem right now?" That's a problem you can solve with a lead magnet.

A lead magnet is a short, digestible, nicely designed example of your work. It might be a PDF, an MP3, an interactive course, or a video series. The right kind of lead magnet will build you an email list of potential customers who all face the same problem. If you design your lead magnet to solve a small problem well, you can demonstrate your expertise, qualify your leads, and build trust with people to whom you can sell in the future.

Lead magnets let people try you before they buy you.

A lead magnet is like the free samples we discussed in chapter 7. At the grocery store, as you walk through the aisles shopping for things to eat, someone might ask if you'd like to try some guacamole. They don't ask you to invest in their avocado farm. They give you a small, non-threatening sample first. And if you like it, you can become a customer. This may not solve your bigger problem of being hungry, but it does solve the smaller problem of finding something tasty to eat.

Nobody puts rotten avocados into their guacamole free sample. That's because people have learned that a lead magnet is created to be the best example of your work.

What Should Your Lead Magnet Be About?

The smallest solvable problem makes the best lead magnet.

If you regurgitate everything you know about a topic, you'll overwhelm someone looking for a simple solution. Offer only the vital information that someone needs to fix a small problem. Then, when they need someone to fix a bigger problem they can't handle themselves, they'll come to you first.

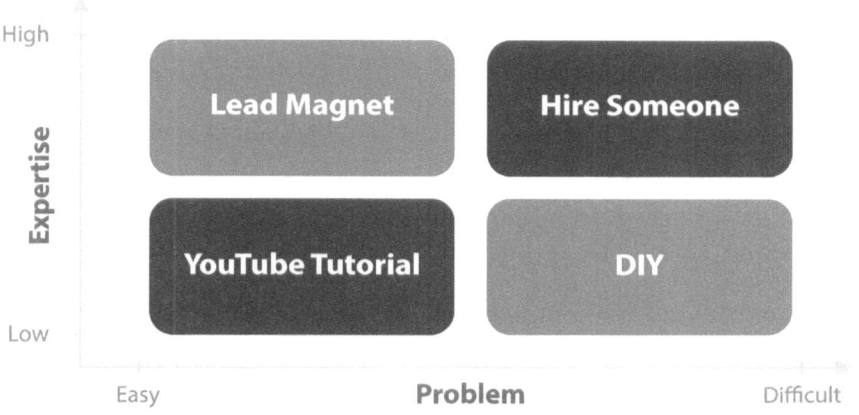

Simple problems are easier to solve than difficult problems. But how do you find someone who can solve a big, complicated problem for you? You test them with a simple problem, that's how.

Before you go into surgery, it's good to see how your doctor puts on a band-aid. If your doctor doesn't know how to bandage a minor wound, would you really trust them with fixing a major wound? You can test your doctor's bedside manner with a verbal consultation. You'll see firsthand her ability to answer your questions and listen to your concerns. That can often be more important to your doctor selection process than knowing how well they perform in the operating room.

The same goes for you and what you sell. People will decide to invest in your bigger solutions based on how well you solve a small problem for them. Help your future customers get to know you by solving a small, specific problem. This will increase their trust and their likelihood of buying from you.

Lead Magnet Case Study 1 — Classical Guitar Shed

Allen Mathews knows his customer avatar really well. They're generally men over 50, and they played a lot of guitar when they were younger. When they try picking up their guitar again, they find they need some help with the basics, so they turn to Google. They search for things like: "warming up for classical guitar," "how to play pairs of notes," and "free guitar sheet music."

These keywords lead to Allen's website ClassicalGuitarShed.com. After providing a long, in-depth tutorial, earning the trust of his reader, Allen offers a lead magnet with the headline "Free Ebook: The 7 Steps to Learn Any Piece Quickly and Easily."

For guitarists who are learning new songs, this is exactly the kind of problem they want to solve. If they don't subscribe, Allen nudges them with a pop-up and a second lead magnet called "30 Fun and Easy(ish) Pieces for Classical Guitar."

These lead magnets have built Allen an email list of guitarists, and he sells his membership program to this audience. He doesn't sell to strangers at the train station or to randos on Twitter. He doesn't want a list of non-guitarists. Allen builds an audience of qualified leads and sells them what they want.

Lead Magnet Case Study 2 — Derek Murphy

Derek Murphy designs book covers. His customer avatar is clearly defined: an author has written a book, and they need a cover designed, so they hire someone like Derek.

Derek knows his audience very well because he's an author himself. He's been through both traditional and self-publishing, so he can talk to his audience knowledgeably about the different options. When you get to Derek's website at creativindie.com, you see his free guide, *Guerilla Publishing*, in the sidebar.

This lead magnet builds Derek a list of authors who want to self-publish their book. He's generous with his expertise, which builds trust with his audience. He even created a free 3D book cover tool so anyone can quickly make a good-looking image for their website. When an author on Derek's list needs to get their book cover designed — or has a friend asking for a recommendation — Derek is the designer they Know, Like, and Trust.

Upsell From Your Lead Magnet

As I mentioned, every lead magnet should solve a problem small enough that your audience doesn't want to hire someone else to fix it, but complicated enough that they can't do it without a bit of research.

So, at the end of your lead magnet, it's smart to sell something. It could be an inexpensive online course, or it could be a free phone call to discuss an expensive program. The final page of your free PDF is ideal for a promotional advertisement for something else you offer. If you close out your lead magnet with "Thanks! See you around the internet," you've wasted an easy opportunity to convert a stranger into a customer.

Attention is a valuable resource. If you have someone's attention online, that means that they have:

✦ Discovered you online

✦ Consumed some of your content

✦ Decided your lead magnet was valuable

✦ Given you their email address to access it

✦ Read through your lead magnet until the end

These people are qualified leads. They've qualified themselves because they face the problems your customers face, and they've shown themselves to be willing to share their contact details with you. An email subscriber who downloads your lead magnet to solve their problem is much more likely than the general populace to buy from you. They've gone three steps forward in the 4-Step Marketing Cycle — they Know you, they Like you, and they Trust you. You know what comes next.

So, ask people to Buy from you in your lead magnet. The call to action can be simple: book a call, or look at my rates, or buy this small product. But if you don't end every lead magnet with a CTA, you're literally leaving money on the table.

A lead magnet is a risk-free method to try one of your solutions. If you solve a small problem well enough, your customer will hire you to solve bigger problems. When people facing a big problem have searched for a small solution, they should find you. This will put you on the short list of people they're willing to pay to fix the larger problem. Through your lead magnet, you've already become their teacher and advisor.

Lead magnet design checklist

- ✦ Your lead magnet addresses a problem your customer avatar faces
- ✦ The title is clear and descriptive (and maybe a little clickbait-y)
- ✦ The medium is quickly digestible (a five-page report is better than a seven-hour video series)
- ✦ Delivery of the lead magnet is automated through your email service provider
- ✦ The lead magnet ends with a call to action to move to the next stage of your Value Ladder

- ✦ Set up a simple landing page that describes the benefits and outcomes of your solution

- ✦ Install a form that requires an email address before they can access the lead magnet

- ✦ Offer the link to the landing page in communities where your customers congregate

The community forums are the ponds, and your lead magnet is the bait.

Fill the Gaps in the Value Ladder

To coordinate all your offers and systems, the Value Ladder Workbook uses an easy, step-by-step process to list out everything you can offer and sell. This workbook helps organize the categories of your Value Ladder. When you know what goes where, you can decide what you can do to ascend people, step by step.

If you notice a gap in your Value Ladder — there is no tripwire or nothing in the Free – Private category to offer to new email subscribers — consider moving an item from a different step, up or down. It's often this revision of offers and content that helps us discover a system that works.

Do you have some old content lying around that would make a great tripwire? An old online course that's no longer selling? A recording of a presentation? Anything you've used as a lead magnet in the past could work. Put a price tag on it and deliver it automatically to your newest email subscribers.

Smart marketing systems are full of authentic messaging that converts strangers into customers automatically. Scope out your own Value Ladder and then sell upward, one step at a time.

ACTION STEPS FOR ELEVATING YOUR PLATFORM

Complete the exercises in the Cornerstone Workbooks at MarketingYourselfBook.com/workbooks:

SCAN ME

1. List everything you offer — free and paid, cheap and expensive, now and in the future — in the Value Ladder Workbook.

2. Divide these offers into the different sections of the workbook.

3. Arrange each list in an order that makes sense — most effective, most potential, most complete, or in order of production.

4. Identify a progression from free to high-priced, where one customer avatar would start with a free offer and work their way up, step by step, to the high-priced offer.

5. Identify any gaps in the progression and plan to fill those gaps.

6. Make sure every asset is promoting something one step higher on the Value Ladder, either through a closing promotion or an automated email follow-up.

7. Do some of these steps on your Value Ladder stand out as more successful or effective? Do some of them need to be retired? Plan your strategy here.

Chapter 16

Statistics for Success

Success is not a mystery. It is a science.

— John Assaraf

When I turned 30, I got a proper grown-up job where I could cosplay as a normie. I wore a tie to work every day as a car insurance sales- man. After a lifetime in theatre, spending my time with artists and creatives, corporate culture was weird. I figured, wearing a tie is just another costume, so I chose the loudest and wackiest ties and leaned into it. I made decent money, but I was very unenthusiastic about what I was selling.

I don't like cars very much. They just get me from place to place. I was even more unenthusiastic about insurance — it's a bunch of paper- work, after all. Lots of my customers thought about their car insurance the same way. They didn't really like insurance; they just knew they needed to have it. Setting up or changing car insurance was treated as an irritating chore.

How can you sell something that you don't care about to people who don't care about it? Well, I found a way to succeed as an insurance salesman by marketing myself with a funny email newsletter.

Every week, I sent my list a weekly newsletter with the details of a ridiculous hypothetical situation. The subject line of every newsletter started with, "Oh, NO!" and then described the risk of some outlandish scenario. Some of my most popular issues were: "Oh, NO! I've fallen from an AIRPLANE without a parachute!" and "Oh, NO! I have to win a fight with an OCTOPUS!" In each newsletter, I provided a humorous, step-by-step solution for how to handle that week's bizarre event.

Every issue also included a few recurring sections: Quote of the Week, This Day in History, and a call to action. The CTA at the end was always the same. At the bottom of every newsletter, I wrote, "If you need to talk to someone about your car insurance, please get in touch with me."

Every single week, somebody replied to my newsletter. Since it had made them laugh, I was the one they contacted when they had to handle their irritating chore. I won sales awards, supported my family, and grew a career — because I built an email list. My company-sponsored website didn't close any sales for me, but emails brought me new customers every week.

Websites Are Like Brochures, While Emails Are Sales Pitches

A brochure does not make a sale. A brochure gives basic information about your business and your offer. As a side effect, it can lend you a layer of credibility. If you spend the time and the effort to make a good brochure (or a good website), your business looks legitimate to new people. This is known as "sales collateral."

Sales collateral does not close a deal. Collateral can increase the likelihood that you can close a deal, but by itself, it doesn't drive revenue.

If your website is your digital brochure, an email is the digital sales pitch. Emails have urgency, because they're time-specific. Emails make offers, and those offers are supported by your digital collateral.

If you can send someone to your website from an email, that's the virtual equivalent of putting your brochure on their desk. Both of these have their place in the sales process. So long as you don't get them confused, you won't confuse your customer.

For my car insurance business, the size of my email list became a growing asset that could predict my success. All I had to do was measure the metrics that mattered — the number of calls I made, emails I sent, quotes I gave, and policies I sold — and that would reveal where I could apply pressure on my systems for the maximum effect.

The Recipe for New Business

Pavlova, a delicate seasonal dessert in New Zealand, is made with eight ingredients: eggs, sugar, vanilla extract, white vinegar, corn flour, cream, strawberries, and kiwis. If I gave you a shopping list, you could buy everything that goes into pavlova. But you wouldn't know how to make it.

To make pavlova, you don't just need eggs. What you really need is beaten egg whites. The fruit goes on the outside, not the inside, and it has to be sliced thinly. The time in the oven is critical, and the order of the steps can make or break the dessert. The instructions to prepare the recipe are just as important as the ingredients themselves.

Most websites are just a list of ingredients. They have a homepage, an about page, a contact form, and some photos. Maybe there's a blog with a few old articles. You could find links to social media profiles and a description of services and rates. After setting up the basics, people get frustrated that their website doesn't bring them leads right away.

It's because they only provide a list of ingredients to the user, and not the whole recipe.

A good recipe tells you how to combine the ingredients to make them into a meal. You have to know how to combine flour, water, tomato sauce, and cheese in a specific recipe, or you'll never make a pizza. A recipe provides specific, step-by-step instructions that allow even inexperienced cooks to succeed.

Your customer could be buying what you sell for the first time in their lives. Make yourself easy to buy. Clear, step-by-step instructions that accompany all the ingredients they need enable new customers to follow your recipe on how to do business with you.

Signal vs. Noise

A website visit is not likely to convert into a sale immediately, but what it can do is begin a relationship. That relationship may lead to a sale, eventually. The relationship doesn't happen on your website — it only starts there. According to HubSpot's market research, 96% of first-time website visitors aren't ready to buy, and 48% of businesses say that most of their leads require long-cycle nurturing.[1]

You can add content all day long to your website, but if it doesn't help a stranger become a customer, it's just contributing to the noise.

As of this writing, every day on the internet, there are:

+ 2 million blog posts created

+ 294 billion emails sent

+ 864,000 hours of video uploaded

+ 400 million tweets tweeted

The average person on the internet is exposed to upwards of 5,000 ads a day, according to the New York Times.[2] That is a lot of noise.

When you go to market with what you're selling, everybody doesn't care.
— Seth Godin

Imagine you're standing in a stadium full of cheering fans. But instead of yelling support for a team on the field, everyone is trying to get

---

1   Allie Vanden Heuvel, "5 Ways to Nurture Leads Through the Sales Process, eCommerce Style," Blogs, HubSpot, last modified February 1, 2017, https://blog.hubspot.com/insiders/lead-nurturing-tips

2   Louise Story, "Anywhere the Eye Can See, It's Likely to See an Ad," New York Times, January 15, 2007, https://www.nytimes.com/2007/01/15/business/media/15everywhere.html/

the attention of everyone else in the stadium. That's what it's like to market yourself on the internet today. The competition for attention is fierce, coming from everyone, everywhere.

WEBSITE SALES FUNNEL

Page	Stage	Reaction
/home	Stranger	What is this about?
/about	Browser	Who is this?
/blog	Reader	This is interesting.
/subscribe	Subscriber	I'll opt-in.
/thanks	Student	Wow, this is good.
/members	Advocate	I should share this.
/store	Customer	I should buy this.

Each page on your website can create an emotional reaction in your reader that encourages them to go to the next stage of the funnel. Create content on each of these pages to incite the emotional reaction in the graphic above. You don't need fancy software or expensive designers. You just need a simple progression for future customers to follow.

Then you need one more critical ingredient: people.

An Email List Collects Future Clients Into One Place

The best method you can use to communicate your offers to your audience is not your website, your business card, or your brochure. Those are static. Email is dynamic. Gaining subscribers on an email list is like filling seats in your own personal auditorium. Everyone who enters is willing to listen to you.

Emailing people who already know you is much different than advertising to strangers, which is more like having a sideshow. "Step right up, come over here, and listen to me!" is how you try to carve out an audience from a crowd, by distracting them into paying attention to you.

With an email list, you have everyone's attention already. People are sitting in your auditorium. Everyone who has subscribed is willing to pay attention to what you have to say. They don't need to be convinced to listen to you. They know you, and if they haven't unsubscribed yet, then they like you, too. Subscribing to your email list is an act of trust.

These people have already completed the first three steps in the 4-Step Marketing Cycle: Know, Like, and Trust. Your email subscribers are those people who are statistically more likely to buy from you than anyone else on the internet.

> *If I have one regret as a business owner, it's not focusing on building our email list earlier in the process.*
>
> — Joe Pulizzi

As of this writing, emails convert better than any other online activity. Fifty-eight percent of adults check their email first thing in the morning, before doing anything else, and 80% of decision-makers prefer to get information about a product or service through a series of articles, rather than an advertisement. If you can set up a good email welcome series, you can educate your customer into doing business with you, and that's a lot more powerful than running an advertisement that your prospect sees once, and then forgets.

If you want proof that email is a good investment, here's a truly startling statistic: for every $1 spent on email, according to Campaign Monitor, there's an average of a $44 return on investment.[3] Building your email list expands your audience and provides you with a base of customers you can sell to. The size and activity of your email list is a practical measurement of your marketing effectiveness.

---

3 *"2016 Year in Review," Campaign Monitor, accessed April 28, 2022, https://www. campaignmonitor.com/company/annual-report/2016/*

Common Marketing Metrics to Measure:

Now, let's talk numbers. The active choices people make through your customer journey can be measured as a percentage rate. How many people go from Step One to Step Two? The conversion ratio represents a number that you can measure over a specific period of time — monthly, daily, yearly, or per campaign.

1. How often does website traffic subscribe to your newsletter? That's your first metric: (Website Traffic) / (Email Subscribers) = **Subscribe Rate**

2. How often do those email subscribers open your email? That's your second metric: (Total Subscribers) / (Email Opens) = **Open Rate**

3. How often do those email subscribers click on an email? That's your third metric: (Total Subscribers) / (Email Clicks) = **Click Rate**

4. Out of everyone who clicked on your email, how many of them made a purchase, booked a call, or completed the goal of the page? Your fourth metric is: (Email Clicks) / (Purchases) = **Purchase Rate**

Here's an example of how these formulas work:

If you have a subscription rate of 10%, that means that with website traffic of 4,000 people, you could expect 400 to subscribe to your email newsletter. After 10 months, you'd have a list of 4,000 subscribers. To keep the numbers simple, let's say you have an open rate of 10%. That means that 400 people on your list of 4,000 open it.

If you make an offer, and 10% of those readers click through at a rate of 1% of the list size, that means 40 people see your offer. If 10% of those people buy, then with a list size of 4,000 people, you can expect to make four sales from one email.

These numbers and ratios will be different for your business and your audience. To find out what these numbers are for you, set up a simple spreadsheet to collect the data. (Or use one of mine, in the Workbooks.)

Leads are the metric that, as marketers, we rely on.
Because leads mean money.

— Kipp Bodnar

Track Your Data, Analyze Your Effectiveness

After you start tracking the data of your systems, you can start pulling the levers. Once you know your conversion ratios — from stranger to browser, from follower to subscriber, from subscriber to customer — you can double any conversion ratio to double your results.

LIST BUILDING

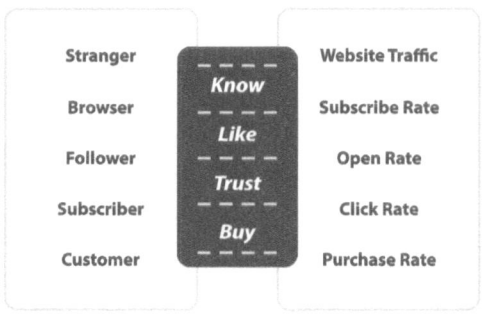

If you double your click rate, for example, and all other numbers stay constant, you'll double your revenue. On the other hand, if you double your website traffic instead, or your subscription rate, the end result will still double. If we assume that all the other conversion ratios stay constant, then doubling any conversion ratio will double your end result.

Growing a list of customers is an advantage that compounds over time. Compound interest is more effective the longer it's in play. The sooner you start, the sooner you can start seeing dramatic results. "Every person I've talked to who has an email list now," says Noah Kagan, founder of App Sumo, "always says, 'I wish I would have started sooner.'"

Have you started yet?

Success is a numbers game, so measure your numbers. Once every three months, you can measure specific metrics, like new leads, new subscribers, and new customers. There are plenty of other metrics you can measure, and some of them might need to be reviewed monthly, weekly, or even daily.

Recording and reviewing the metrics that matter to your business growth will help you align your strategy to your goals.

ACTION STEPS FOR ELEVATING YOUR PLATFORM

SCAN ME

Complete the exercises in the Cornerstone Workbooks at MarketingYourselfBook.com/workbooks:

1. Make a copy of the Marketing Metrics Dashboard.

2. Add a row for any metric you want to track.

3. Collect data every month and add to the dashboard.

4. Review the data every month with someone who can provide strategic advice.

5. Set goals for your future numbers.

6. Identify the activities it will take to achieve those goals.

7. Schedule a date and time to do those activities.

Epilogue

Most funnels don't work when you launch them. Even if you're a pro, it may take two, three, four, or ten tries until you get it right.

— Julie Stoian

Marketing yourself is like brewing a cup of coffee.

The coffee you drink, as invigorating and existential as it is, starts out completely different from what ends up in your cup. Coffee begins life as a hard, greenish bean, and it doesn't look (or smell) remotely edible. Coffee is not a food. Humans cannot digest it. But somehow, we found a way to love it.

Originally, the coffee plant evolved caffeine as a poison, to prevent small insects from eating its berries. Fortuitously, the poison dosage in the coffee plant is not lethal to primates 10,000 times the size of insects. Instead, caffeine consumption gives us psychoactive effects. This mood-altering drug can enhance our attention, increase our productivity, and stimulate our creativity.

The process for getting this drug out of an inedible coffee bean is intense. I'm astounded that our ancestors were able to discover this process. First, you have to burn the bean — but not a lot. You only roast it. If you burn the coffee bean so much that it catches on fire, then it becomes char and ash. But if you roast it slowly, getting it sort of burnt (but not really burnt), then you have completed the first step in the lengthy process of making coffee.

Next, you have to:

- ✦ grind this roasted bean into a powder
- ✦ mix it with boiling water, and then
- ✦ strain all the ground roasted coffee beans out of the liquid.

By the end of this complicated potion-making process, the original material you started with is completely gone. A cup of coffee doesn't resemble its source material at all. Marketing yourself is the same. You start with different materials than what you deliver. What you make will be subjected to a complex and esoteric process to create something completely new. It may end up nothing like what you started with, but it's been flavored by what you've done.

Marketing Yourself Is a Series of Failed Experiments

I want you to think of the Workbooks that accompany this book like brewing coffee. Your first draft is a raw bean, and it needs to be ripened, and plucked, and aged, and roasted, and ground, and boiled, and strained ... it won't be pretty. You'll make a lot of mistakes and run into a lot of dead ends. That's okay; it's part of the process.

Do you think the first cup of coffee ever made came out delicious? Or were there many failed attempts on the search to discover this magical brew? The hard truth is: a lot of your marketing will not work. When you first try a new message or a new campaign, it's not going to be perfect. It might not even be close. If you've launched a campaign that went nowhere, welcome to the club!

An unfortunate truth of marketing is that it's a lot of guesswork. You can find your way through a maze by sheer luck, guessing at every turn. Or you can be systematic and methodical about your experiments. Before spending a bunch of money on an advertising campaign, for example, it's wise to experiment with your messaging in a small market first, with a small budget. Then you can measure variations of your messaging to see what's most effective, before committing more dollars.

The good news is that every marketing failure teaches you a lesson about your business, your audience, and the journey from stranger to customer. You may delete those failed sales pages from your website and throw that old stack of brochures in the recycling bin. But like the coffee grounds that were strained out of your coffee, all of those failed experiments will flavor your marketing in the future.

Only Testing Will Tell

Every marketing initiative takes time and resources away from the core functions of your business. The worst part is that you can spend all this time and effort on marketing, and you don't even know if it will be successful! But the same is true with pasta. You'll never discover if your spaghetti is ready until you boil it in water, simmer it for a while, and then check it. Many people throw spaghetti against the wall to test its readiness. If it sticks, it's ready. If it's not, let it boil a little longer.

To get the perfect texture, you need to remove your spaghetti before it turns to mush. You have to check too early. You need to fail experiments.

By the time you sit down for a meal of pasta, you don't even remember those failed experiments. You threw some spaghetti against the wall, and you did it too early. The spaghetti didn't stick. So you kept up the heat, stirred the pot, and tried again. Eventually, you made a wonderful meal.

If you want to do anything well,
you have to be willing to do it badly, first.

Guide Your Business by Experiments

Marketing yourself is a combination of messaging, lead generation, and experiments.

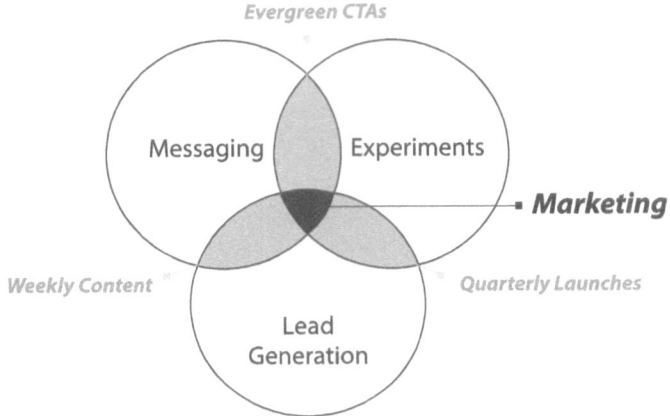

After you create some content to share, some people may like, comment, or subscribe. Others won't. The quality of attention we receive can be just as important as the frequency of attention. Based on the resonance of your messaging experiments, you can measure what's effective.

> ### Good marketing is the art of giving, gaining, and directing attention.

You could only create content that you like, with no regard for what your audience likes, but the effectiveness of your marketing will be limited. Pay attention to what resonates with your audience and modify your future messages to align with their responses. What you think will work is often different than what actually works.

> *Half the money I spend on advertising is wasted;*
> *the trouble is I don't know which half.*
>
> — John Wanamaker

Epilogue

You can blanket the world with messages and try to guess what's working. Or you can methodically test in small segments to identify what works best.

You probably won't get it right on the first try. Just keep experimenting with messaging until something begins to work. Failing experiments, reviewing your activity, and making new strategic decisions — that's how you iterate. As you improve the cornerstones of your marketing, your platform will elevate over time.

The Four Levels of Platforms

What I've seen over the years, helping experts and entrepreneurs grow their businesses, is that there are four levels of platforms. By working on your cornerstones, your platform naturally progresses through these four levels:

Level 1: The Soapbox

Anyone can get on a soapbox, so long as you have something to say. Once you get anyone to pay attention to you, you have a platform. On a soapbox, you might be ignored by most of the people who pass you by, but you're elevated above the crowd, sharing a message that matters to you.

Level 2: The Showroom

In a showroom, what you say focuses on what you sell. In a showroom, people voluntarily come to you to listen to your pitch. A showroom is explicitly for commerce, displaying the different offers you have available, and providing all the relevant information to make a buying decision.

Level 3: The Stage

When you're on a stage, what you say attracts a crowd. You don't have to collect the crowd yourself because you can create relationships with the leaders and custodians of other audiences. By getting in front of large numbers of people, sharing your message, and shining your light, your systems do the selling for you, transitioning your work from making the sale to educating the market.

Level 4: The Stadium

In a stadium, what you say changes the market. You're one of the leaders in your field, and the strategic decisions you make will create ripple effects on the platforms of others. Every event is a big event, and you can invite opening acts to bring their audiences to you.

Each of these four levels has its own set of problems.

The Problem With a Soapbox:

A soapbox is not commercially viable. You volunteer your time on a soapbox, while you get paid for your time in a showroom.

The Problem With a Showroom:

A showroom has a ceiling. You can only fit so many people inside a showroom, and those people have to be convinced to enter.

The Problem With a Stage:

A stage requires touring. No one audience can support a larger platform for very long; your work is to continually find new audiences to befriend, to educate, and to convert into your own systems. Without continuous new traffic, your platform can become oversized and cumbersome.

The Problem With a Stadium:

A stadium is so big, you have to increase your focus. With so many opportunities available, what you decline becomes more important than what you accept. A stadium-level platform has greater risk of becoming unbalanced, and because it's so high, there is farther to fall.

Epilogue

Universal Solution for All Platforms

Even though the four levels of platforms have different problems, the solutions all require the same four cornerstones: your Positioning, your Profit, your Strategy, and your Systems.

When you want to elevate your platform, chances are that some of your cornerstones are higher than others. Spend three months working diligently on one cornerstone, starting with the one that needs the most attention, before moving on to the others.

Questions you can ask yourself about your platform include:

- ✦ **Is it visible?** Can people see your platform from afar? What's in the way, that prevents you from being seen?

- ✦ **Is it interesting? Will people find your** platform intriguing? **Have they been looking for something just like this?**

- ✦ **Is it valuable?** How do you compare to everyone else? Do you give a positive exchange of time, money, joy, attention, reputation, or inspiration?

- ✦ **Is it stable?** Would misfortune topple you to the ground? How well can you handle the unexpected? Do you feel safe up there?

Raising Your Cornerstones Elevates Your Platform

By focusing this book on each of these four cornerstones in turn, I hope the concepts I've shared can help you create a personal platform that elevates you above the crowd. When you earn the attention of an audience that's willing to pay you for your expertise, you can sustain your livelihood from that relationship. With the right systems and strategy supporting you, all you have to do is show up and shine.

Acknowledgments

Thanks to the clients and customers who trusted me to help improve their personal platform. Our work together is what created this book.

Thanks to Daniel Stein, for teaching me the coffee lecture, pantomime, and many valuable lessons about becoming a good man.

Thanks to Kim Ledgerwood, for helping me to find the right word.

Thanks to Matt Church and Peter Cook, for teaching me the Foundation program, and introducing me to a community of people I aspire to be.

Thanks to Lisa O'Neill, for leading that community of Thought Leaders into the digital Immersions so enthusiastically.

Thanks to Sharí Alexander, for being my outside eye, and keeping my sight true to my vision.

Thanks to Brant and Eric, for filling the brother-shaped holes in my heart.

Thanks to my kids, for laughing & learning with me, and for bouncing on the trampoline with me in the middle of the day.

And most of all, thanks to my lady wife. Johanna, I am grateful every day for the care and love you give to our family. You are the shining star we all revolve around.

Afterword

If you've found this book helpful, please share it with other experts and entreprneurs you encounter along your own journey.

Here are a few things you can do right now:

1. Write an honest review of this book and post it on Amazon or Goodreads

2. Subscribe to my newsletter at https://CaelanHuntress.com/subscribe

3. Share c selfie photo of you and this book on **#MarketingYourselfBook** and tag @caelanhuntress to say hello on social media.

Best of luck to you! Have fun out there.

About the Author

Caelan Huntress started his career as an acrobat in the circus, earning and maintaining the attention of an audience as a street performer. He applies those lessons to the field of marketing, where he earns and maintains the attention of a demographic.

Caelan is a dynamic speaker, trainer, and business coach, who combines his skills as a theatrical performer and technical nerd to make compelling virtual experiences. He is a Certified Inbound Marketer through HubSpot, a Certified Direct Response Copywriter through Digital Marketer, and a Certified Virtual Host through eSpeakers. He lives with his wife and three children in Aotearoa New Zealand.